Teaching Styles and Pupil Progress

NEVILLE BENNETT

with

Joyce Jordan
George Long
Barbara Wade

Foreword by Jerome Bruner

Harvard University Press
Cambridge, Massachusetts
1976

Library of Congress Catalog Card Number 76-40500
ISBN 0-674-87095-6

Printed in the United States of America

Contents

Acknowledgements

Although written by one person the book represents the efforts of many: notably Professor Noel Entwistle who co-directed the investigation, and Joyce Jordan, George Long and Barbara Wade who were, for varying lengths of time, employed as Research Officers. But many others provided invaluable assistance. Sheila Hargreaves and Sue Bennett undertook such arduous and thankless tasks as marking tests, keeping and checking records, and preparing data for computer analysis. A number of research students also played their part. The analyses of Monique Statham and Ian Honeyford are included in chapter 7, and that of Marcia Applebee in chapter 3. Elaine Anthony and Judith Crompton shared the joy of typing the manuscript.

A special word of gratitude is extended to all those teachers who responded to the original questionnaire, and more particularly to the thirty-seven teachers who gave the research team every cooperation in the second stage of the inquiry. Without these, and without the generous financial support of the Social Science Research Council, the study could not have been carried out.

Finally, acknowledgements are due to Professor Robert Soar of the University of Florida for permission to include figure 2.2; to Holt, Rinehart and Winston for permission to reproduce figure 2.1 from 'The Study of Teaching' by Dunkin and Biddle (1974); and to Professor Ned Flanders for allowing the reproduction of his interaction analysis schedule in table 2.1.

The foreword by Jerome Bruner is adapted, with permission, from a review in *New Society*, April 29, 1976.

Foreword

JEROME BRUNER
Watts Professor of Psychology
University of Oxford

The gap between doctrinal positions in teaching and the evidence required to support or refute them is notorious. It is a gap that has been explained in a variety of ways, all of them reasonable, none of them compelling. Yet if educational practice is to achieve any rationality, and is to be freed of its addiction to passing fashions, we shall need a more regular assessment of how yesterday's enthusiasms are faring in the cold light of today. Neville Bennett's book sets out to do this.

One thing that makes such an assessment particularly difficult is the curious habit, in educational philosophers, of obliterating the distinction between means and ends—that is, between what we wish to achieve and how to go about achieving it. I rather suspect that it is not just 'loose thinking' that produces this confusion, but something deeper, something structural. For it is striking that the means proposed by educational theorists are often miniature versions of the ends they seek. Ends *become* means.

Nowhere is this plainer than in the modern statement of 'progressive' education. So, for example, the Plowden Report of 1967 borrows from the Hadow Report of 1931 the stirring battle cry: 'The curriculum is to be thought of in terms of activity and experience rather than knowledge to be acquired and facts to be stored.' So what, then, is the object of education? The achievement of rich experience and activity, of course. Indeed, the emphasis in Hadow (echoed 36 years later in Plowden) had so fused the cart with the horse that it is impossible to sort them out even abstractly.

Take this sample, quoted by Neville Bennett: 'The school is not merely a teaching shop, it must transmit values and attitudes. It is a community in which children learn to live first and foremost as children and not as future adults. The school sets

vii

out deliberately to devise the right environment for children to allow them to be themselves, and to develop in a way and at the pace appropriate for them. It lays special stress on individual discoveries, on firsthand experience, and on opportunities for creative work. It insists that knowledge does not fall into neatly separate compartments and that work and play are not opposite but complementary.'

And in a burst of what can only be called moral indignation it proclaims, 'Any practice which predetermines the pattern and imposes it upon all is to be discouraged.' What about spelling? The inexorable constraints of simultaneous equations? The structure of tragedy, or the contrasting balance of human myths? Are these to be banned? And how shall the core of the culture be transmitted? What kinds of adult do Plowden and Hadow have in mind?

Part of the means-end muddle, I think, relates to implicit theories held by laymen, educationist and philosopher alike, about the impact of experience in the early years on experience later in life. It is reflected most clearly in the progressive refrain that education is to be considered as life itself, and not as a preparation for later living. It is a view that risks being blind to the subtle course of the human life cycle, and the subtle and indirect ways in which the child becomes father to the man. The issues, rather, have to do with a constant assessment of what, in fact, our practices are doing to children whom we commit to educational institutions. Though we may grant the difficulty of assessing the relation between means and ends, the only way out of the muddle is to examine the effects of what we are doing, how we are arranging schooling, and with what results. Curiously, there is very little hard data to guide such efforts. Sensitive and tough-minded investigations on methods of instruction are needed.

It is against this background that Bennett's book should be read. For it is that rare kind of study that sets itself the explicit task of disentangling educational means from educational objectives, and it proceeds with a dispassionate skill to combine conceptual subtlety with empirical open-mindedness. The result is a powerful, disturbing book that is bound to reverberate in educational and political debate over the coming years. It sets out to examine the range of teaching styles from the formal, teacher-centered, controlled classroom at one extreme to the informal, more open plan, student-centered one at the other; and it inquires into the strengths and weaknesses of each. It takes as background the controversy between the adherents of the progressive ideal on the one side and the traditional formalists on the other.

Bennett and his colleagues posed two sets of questions: (a) Do various teaching styles differentially affect the intellectual and emotional growth of pupils? (b) Do different types of pupils perform better under certain teaching styles than others?

The main findings can be summed up quickly. The more formal the teaching, the more time pupils spend working on the subject matter at hand. And in general, though with some important exceptions, the more time pupils spend working on a subject, the more they improve at it—not a huge surprise, but one that grows in importance as one looks at the other results. For though it may come as no revelation that students in the more formal classrooms improved considerably more in reading and in mathematical skills than the less formally taught, it is much more revealing that pupils in informal settings did *not* do any better on their creative writing than their more formally instructed fellows.

What of personality and teaching styles? Most pupil 'types' progress better under more formal teaching. And particularly the insecure and neurotic pupil: he seems able to attend to work better, and harder, in a formal setting. Particularly for the unstable child, the informal setting seems to invite time-wasting activities—indeed, the 'unmotivated', rather neurotic child, was found to work four times as much at his studies in a formal setting than in an informal one. Interestingly enough, the informal class seems to increase favourable attitudes towards school—but it also increases anxiety. And for the 'timid' pupil the informal classroom brings him out socially though it does not increase the quality of his work as much as the formal setting does.

There are some anomalies in the findings. The scholastically less able boy is hindered least by the informal classroom, though he still performs worse than his formally-instructed fellows. Interestingly enough, the ones who suffer most in scholastic performance in informal class teaching are the ablest students. Inadvertently, informal classrooms are academic levellers, though it was thought they would allow all to proceed at their own pace. They also—again inadvertently—hurt most the less well-adjusted student who, it was thought, would be most helped.

Informal teaching seems to have hindered the transmission of skills of literacy and numeracy. And it has not succeeded in compensating for this loss by altering creativity, or by buttressing insecure personalities in any measurable way—save through increasing identification with school. But at the same time it has created anxiety over unstructuredness. Teachers report, moreover, that informal teaching is considerably more demanding than formal and runs the risk, when it misfires, of failing to teach anybody anything. In one teacher's words, a formal class is bound to teach somebody something.

There will, of course, be disagreement about the force of Bennett's findings. Statistical analysis is still a controversial art, and no study of this scope, however well conceived, is entirely without flaw. Americans may also wonder whether results from a small area of England have anything meaningful to say about American schools. These are legitimate concerns. However, Bennett's study is sufficiently well designed that it cannot be dismissed on technical grounds, and the effects he observed are so large that they merit serious discussion on both sides of the Atlantic.

Still, it would be unwise for such discussion to leap directly from Bennett's pages into the political fray. Before readers start stacking up points *for* the conservative approach or *against* progressivism, it might be worth looking at the cultural landscape against which Bennett's findings should be viewed. We are just at the end of an era in the human sciences in which concepts of self-direction, self-realisation, and self-reward lived unchallenged in a world where self-determination was the ideal. And indeed, this ideal is central to the democratic concept. But ends and means become confused: What of self-demand feeding schedules for babies? What of the 'innateness hypothesis', in whose name it was insisted that language is discovered and need not be taught? And what of the ever more dominating contemporary cultures of youth? The adult as model or teacher or friend is in eclipse. Common sense and technical inquiry are finally catching up with the romantic excess. It turns out that the mother and her reactions are crucial for language acquisition and that self-demand in feeding and infant care leaves the child without a stable source of reciprocation. New studies are now pointing to the critical role of the adult tutor, in social and intellectual development. Early connection with a supporting world begins to emerge as a *leitmotif* for the development of later self-determination. And indeed, one of the central issues is to assure the dispossessed that this connection is not destroyed by isolating alienation.

There is yet another relevant thread that runs through contemporary work on human development which has to do with the nature and structure of human skills. The exercise of a complex human skill involves mastering constituent sub-skills that can later be combined to solve tougher problems. The heart of the matter is not so much drilling the simpler skills into the young, for that does not assure later 'creativity', but that these are fruitfully combined. It must also involve an opportunity for putting one's own skills together in order to fit the task. Without this chance, there is a scattering of intellectual powers.

Let me end with an example from research on the preschool young, for it illustrates the point. One of the known ways of increasing the young child's capacity to concentrate attention over longer periods of time is to have adults close by who can serve as 'scaffold' for the child, shielding him from distraction, and permitting him to get over the rough places that would put him off. Once the child has experienced these protected, deeper forays into the world, he will increasingly prolong his attention on his own, knowing what to expect. And having done so, he will develop mastery on his own of matters that before, without his newfound powers, would have thrown him. So it may well be that we are at the beginning of an era where, at long last, we will examine what constitutes the heart of teaching. And we would do well to remember that, in the deep evolutionary sense, we are the only species that has ever existed which depends for its adaptation upon teaching.

We do well, then, to read Bennett's book with a certain prudence. Before we brickbat the progressives and throw bouquets to the conservatives, we had better recognise that the art of teaching is little aided by dogmatism among the onlookers. All that we know better by virtue of Bennett's splendid study is that formal classrooms work by virtue of giving more opportunity to the pupil to spend time learning whatever it is that we choose to teach him. We are only at the beginning of understanding how a curriculum equips a learner with the skills and attitudes and values that make him richer, stronger and more critically self-reliant.

The progressives' fallacy was the assumption that you arrive at the terminus immediately—self-directed from the start and not just later. Now we know better. Self-direction is wasteful if one does not know where one is going or why. But to swing back to a Prussian model of authoritarian teaching will only assure that the pendulum will keep going through its dull, historically repetitive trajectory. If Bennett's book succeeds in making both sides of the debate a little more thoughtful about the next steps, it will have earned the honour it richly deserves.

Preface

Teaching methods in primary schools have been the subject of much controversy among educationalists and parents alike, particularly since the publication of the Plowden Report on primary education in 1967. The report welcomed the introduction and proliferation of more progressive methods, with their stress on enhanced pupil choice in work, greater freedom to move and talk, group work, integrated rather than separate subjects and a general diminution in teacher direction and control.

Advocates of this approach claim that it encourages individualised learning, and fosters the social and emotional development of children without detracting from their academic progress. Critics of the approach view the increased freedom of pupils with alarm, fearing that 'progressive' is synonymous with 'permissive', and placing every hint of declining standards firmly at the classroom door of progressive teachers.

Protagonists on both sides fight rhetorically in the pages of the national and educational press, and occasionally the public is treated to a symbolic, or rather semantic, burial of progressivism undertaken by the contributors to the *Black Paper* series. Unfortunately the battle is waged on an emotional plane, assertion countered by further assertion. The only weapon not used appears to be research evidence. There is surprisingly little evidence available and much of this emanates from the United States. The study reported in the following chapters was therefore instigated to provide evidence on such basic pedagogical questions as 'Do teaching methods (or styles as they are called in this book) have a differential effect on the academic progress of pupils?' and 'Do pupils of differing personality characteristics progress similarly when taught by different approaches?' However, there are many other subsidiary questions of interest and these are described in the following summaries of chapter content.

Chapter 1 provides a backcloth to the investigation, emphasising the emotional and assertive nature of the debate. It also traces the cycles of fashion in educational practice in Britain and the United States.

Chapter 2 asks the question 'Do teaching styles make a difference?' and attempts to provide an answer by reviewing the evidence from previous research studies. This is followed by a critique of these studies on which is based the rationale and design of the investigation reported here.

One of the major deficiencies of previous studies is the almost exclusive reliance on gross distinctions between teaching styles whereby all teachers are labelled either progressive or traditional, democratic or authoritarian, informal or formal. Chapter 3 reports a large scale survey of teaching practices in northern England from which a new classification or typology of teaching styles was created. This resulted in not two, but twelve styles. Evidence is then presented on the validity of this typology.

Chapter 4 examines the link between teacher aims and opinions and teaching styles, and provides answers to the following questions. Do teachers who have adopted different styles have different aims, and if so what are they? What are the opinions of, for example, informal teachers on formal methods and vice versa? How strong is the link between opinions about teaching methods and the actual method adopted?

Chapter 5 can be regarded as one of the core chapters since it considers pupil progress over one school year in English, reading and mathematics and relates this to teaching style. Some of the questions considered are: Under which teaching styles do pupils progress most? Do boys progress better than girls? Do high ability pupils progress better under certain teaching styles? And what is the relationship between eleven-plus and progress?

Having established that certain styles do relate to better progress, it is necessary to attempt to ascertain why this should be. In chapter 6 the observed behaviour of pupils in informal and formal classrooms is related to their progress. Of most interest here are the different levels of work activity and pupil interaction observed in the different settings.

In order to broaden the attainment criteria stories were written by pupils and analysed in two ways. One, to test the frequently heard assertion that informal methods foster creative or imaginative writing, and two, to test the view that formal methods result in better standards of punctuation and spelling. These are reported in chapter 7.

Many studies have investigated the link between pupil personality and attainment at school but results have been equivocal. Chapter 8 describes how this link was investigated in this study by grouping pupils together who had similar personality characteristics in order to form pupil types. The progress of different types of pupils was then related to teaching style. Do pupils of the same personality type perform similarly in different types of classroom? Which has the greater effect on progress, teaching style or pupil personality?

Chapter 9 investigates the relationship between pupil personality and behaviour in class. The major question considered here is: Do pupils of the same personality type behave differently in formal and informal classrooms?

Chapter 10 pulls together the evidence contained in earlier chapters to present a coherent pattern. This pattern is, in turn, used to raise issues which, from the data gathered, appear to underlie effective teaching of the basic subjects. It is felt that these issues, such as the amount of time a pupil spends 'on-task', and structure and sequence in the curriculum, are more important than the individual findings, given the methodological and statistical limitations endemic in studies in this very complex area. The reader should therefore beware of making causal inferences where none are possible, or using the evidence to advocate a given teaching approach. Instead, the findings and issues should be used as the basis for considering such basic and challenging questions as: What specific aspects of formal classrooms are responsible for progress in the basic subjects and how can they be successfully incorporated into more informal settings? How can teaching be arranged in elementary schools to provide sufficient structure for the anxious, with enough pressure and stimulation for the brightest, and with encouragement and support for the weaker so as to make learning an enjoyable and rewarding experience for them all? Neither simplistic slogans nor patent 'cure-alls' are likely to provide answers. Sensitive interpretation of research findings provides a sound basis from which dedicated teachers can help pupils of all types learn more effectively regardless of the organisational arrangements adopted in their school.

TEACHING STYLES AND PUPIL PROGRESS

I

Myth and assertion in primary school practice

It could be argued that in an ideal educational world new ideas and techniques would be subjected to objective evaluation before being implemented. But this is not an ideal world and practice often seems to be based on myth and assertion rather than objective evidence. Bloom (1972) was perhaps not too far from the mark when he stated 'In education we continue to be seduced by the equivalent of snake-oil remedies, fake cancer cures, perpetual motion contraptions, and old wives' tales. Myth and reality are not clearly differentiated, and we frequently prefer the former to the latter.' Young (1965) makes a similar point when claiming that there is innovation without research – new ideas based on hunches, never tested objectively; and research without innovation – academic studies which make no impact, and are unintelligible except to other researchers. There are many examples of both types in education, but whereas the latter are fairly harmless the former are more serious in their possible consequences. They occur, according to Cronbach (1966), because of educators' penchants for new fads. 'In education, unfortunately, there is a great furore about whatever is announced as the latest trend, and the schools seem to career erratically after each Pied Piper in turn. This giddy chase keeps them almost beyond earshot of the researcher standing on his tiny, laboriously stamped patch of solid ground, crying in a pathetic voice "Wait for me. Wait for me."'

Cycles of fashion

As far as primary education is concerned this 'giddy chase' has consisted of running round in circles. Education would seem to be as prone to changes in fashion as is clothing, and these cycles of fashion can be perceived most clearly in an examination of changes in teaching and curriculum in the United States since the 1920s. At that time the influence of John Dewey and his followers was making itself felt in the assault on the validity of the conventional conception of what should constitute education. The declarations of Bobbitt and Kilpatrick epitomise the cleavage. 'Education' stated Bobbitt (1924) 'is primarily for adult life, not for child life. Its fundamental responsibility is to prepare for the fifty years of adulthood, not for the twenty years of childhood and youth.' This notion of education as preparation was in stark contrast with Kilpatrick's (1918) dictum that 'education be considered as life itself and not as a mere preparation for later living'.

Conventional schooling was designed to open to pupils the boxes of knowledge symbolised by subjects, drawing on the technology of books and teacher talk, whereas progressive education was an active, discovery-based process with the teacher cast in a guiding, stimulating role rather than a didactic one. Under the impetus of the progressive education movement progressive teaching methods reached their zenith, particularly at elementary level, in the thirties and forties. However, by the late forties and fifties the term shifted from one of praise to one of opprobrium. The exact causes are difficult to ascertain, although they appear to have revolved around criticisms of the quality of teachers and teaching, by parents and scholars alike. Many teachers, it would appear, could not cope. As one biographer of the progressive education movement commented, 'to ask them [teachers] to discard both their traditional methods *and* their subject matter was simply more of an adjustment than most could satisfactorily make' (Graham 1967). Parental criticism, always a more potent factor in the United States than in Britain, was to the effect that traditional education, with a teacher of average endowments, at least left the pupil with a core of information which, unsatisfactory as it might be, was often missing from uninspired progressive teaching. Scholarly criticism, as might be expected, related to the concern that the schools were failing to reflect and incorporate advances in knowledge. It was an attack on intellectual flabbiness. Progressive education had grown soft.

None of this was empirically demonstrated of course, but assertion and myth won the day. Progressive teaching thus fell from favour and entered oblivion for at least two decades whilst the United States trembled at the trauma of Sputnik 1 and, equally traumatic, the era of curriculum development and reform. This era saw a major reorientation of the curriculum development process from reliance on the practitioner in the local school setting to substantial utilisation of expert resources from the scientific and larger educational community. Writing in the early 1960s one Harvard Professor stated 'the decade which began in 1955 . . . may ultimately come to be regarded as one of the major turning points in American public education.' Never before in the history of their schools had Americans been involved in such widespread experimentation.

But this did not relate to the real situation in schools. According to contemporary writers the schools themselves remained largely unaffected, indeed immune from change. Ungraded primary schools, team teaching, instructional television, teacher aides, new curriculum packages, were all put forward and supposedly accepted by schools. But as Goodlad (1969) remarked after assessing the prevalence of ungraded schools, 'I should have known better. I should have realised that teachers and administrators would reach eagerly for the catchy innovative label, and that non-grading would be used to describe pitifully old practices of interclass achievement grouping.' Another ruefully remarked that it is easier to put a man on the moon than change school practices.

From the frustration at this change without change has developed a prevailing climate which is hospitable to fresh alternatives to the 'floundering educational establishment'. One of these fresh alternatives is progressive education, admittedly dressed slightly differently and wearing a trendy new name -- 'open' education. The open education movement is growing rapidly and has given birth to litters of books and articles, all greeting their progenitor as the new educational panacea. The cycle is complete.

The American experience mirrors that in Britain, except that, until very recently, the cycles have been out of phase. In the twenties British schools were still traditional and, despite the promulgation of Dewey's philosophy in the Hadow Report on primary education (1931), remained so until the early sixties. The change from traditional to progressive methods was a slow process based mainly on the commitment of practitioners rather than externally imposed like so many other innovations. This 'chalk face' movement was legitimated by the Plowden Report (1967) which was strongly prescriptive of progressive education. The report reiterated the now famous passage from its predecessor, the Hadow Report of 1931, that 'the curriculum is to be thought of in terms of activity and experience rather than knowledge to be acquired and facts to be stored.' In its formulation of aims it was stated that

the school is not merely a teaching shop, it must transmit values and attitudes. It is a community in which children learn to live first and foremost as children and not as future adults . . . The school sets out deliberately to devise the right environment for children, to allow them to be themselves, and to develop in a way and at the pace appropriate to them . . . It lays special stress on individual discovery, on first hand experience, and on opportunities for creative work. It insists that knowledge does not fall into neatly separate compartments and that work and play are not opposite but complementary.

It argued against rigid division of the curriculum into subjects since these tend to interrupt children's trains of thought and to hinder them from realising the common elements in problem solving. It urged self chosen activity at the expense of class teaching: 'any practice which pre-determines the pattern and imposes it upon all is to be discouraged.' Flexibility was to be encouraged, to make good use of the interest and curiosity of children, to minimise the notion of subject matter being rigidly compartmental, and to allow the teacher to adopt a consultative, guiding, stimulating role rather than a purely didactic one. Project work, centres of interest and integration were suggested, not only as means for allowing time for interests which do not fit neatly under subject headings, but also, and more importantly, for seeing the different dimensions of subject work, and of using the forms of observation and communication which are not suitable to a given sequence of learning. In this context visits outside school were to be encouraged to allow children to experience the immediate environment.

The use of external rewards such as stars and marks as a source of motivation was deprecated: '. . . one of the main educational tasks of primary school is to build on and strengthen children's intrinsic interest in learning and lead them to learn for themselves rather than from a fear of disapproval or desire for praise.' In the kind of school the Plowden Committee envisaged there is little or no need for the stimulus of marks and class places and rewards, or for the sanctions of punishment: 'It can be associated with psychological perversion affecting both beater and beaten . . . After full consideration we recommend that the infliction of physical pain as a recognised method of punishment in primary schools should be forbidden.' Group work, communication between children in class, and non-streaming were also to be encouraged.

The report concluded that 'finding out has *proved* [my emphasis] to be better for children than being told', and that 'the gloomy forebodings of the decline of knowledge which would follow progressive methods have been discredited.' However, a long, hard search through this lengthy report will fail to locate one piece of research cited to support such statements. In fact there appears to be no research reported which relates at all to the effectiveness of differing teaching approaches.

Such whole-hearted and forthright acceptance and approval of the progressive approach produced the inevitable rejoinders. Peters (1969) contended that the philosophy underlying Plowden's aims 'proliferates in important half truths that are pervaded as educational panaceas'. What has happened, he continued, 'is that *a* method for learning some things has become puffed up into *the* method for learning almost anything'; he detected 'a yearning for some overall recipe for teaching. My contention is that no such recipe is possible.'

The publication of a series of *Black Papers* (Cox and Dyson 1969a, 1969b, 1970, 1975) probably represented the backlash effect in its most strident form. Their contributors took a swing at anything labelled progressive, permissive or egalitarian, often using the terms synonymously. The arguments ranged over all levels of education, over academic standards, teaching methods, streaming and the general effects of progressives on society at large.

Progressive education was regarded as the root of all evil. In the editorial of the third *Black Paper* it was stated that 'The results of permissive education can be seen all around us, in the growth of anarchy.' In similar vein, Maude (1969) in the first *Black Paper* lashed the egalitarian (progressive) for disliking class marks and competitive examinations: 'he has a horror of any test which some children might fail. This leads him to decry the importance of academic standards and discipline – and indeed of learning itself. He will advocate a variety of "new teaching methods", which, in fact, absolve anyone from teaching and anyone from having to learn.' Maude finished with a plea for action from all teachers 'to do battle against the enemies within their own gates. The Trojan horse of egalitarianism has already been dragged deep into their citadel.'

Bantock (1969) was concerned about the competence of the progressive teacher: 'Used competently . . . these new methods have a great deal to offer. Used incompetently, as a gimmick or a fashion, they are probably more disastrous to learning than an exclusive reliance on the old formal methods. These methods, with their permissive atmosphere, in the hands of incompetent teachers are enervating and time wasting . . .'

Any educational problem appears to be placed at the door of progressive education by the banner carriers of the traditional right, who blame all adolescent misbehaviour on progressive primary schools. This line of argument often appears when the question of discipline arises. The so-called National Campaign for Discipline in Schools claimed recently that progressive education has over-emphasised child-centredness, and that sentimental egalitarianism has made standards of individual achievement and behaviour irrelevant. 'Children have become less ready to do what they are told. A few rowdy children in a class infect the others, bullies emerge to fill the authority vacuum, and violence, vandalism and arson increase.'

These critics have in turn been taken to task and accused of being polemical journalists, of attacking straw men, and of over-generalising (Johnson and McAthlone 1970; Rubinstein and Stoneman 1970). However, it is interesting to note that the original assertion was only countered by further assertion, a development which highlights a disturbing facet of contemporary educational discourse. A problem is perceived, but instead of being researched objectively, and possible causes and consequences being assessed, 'enemies' are chosen for attack, often irrationally. Suspects are identified and proven guilty without evidence or trial, a process that is hardly likely to enhance the quality of educational debate or practice. In the absence of such evidence prejudice rather than reason has prevailed, and a term such as 'progressive' has become less a word descriptive of a certain mode of teaching, and more a slogan or catch word which according to Richards (1974) is either brandished fervently or repudiated violently depending on the disputant's position.

Defenders of the traditional faith have been cited most, simply because they tend to air their views more frequently. As Johnson (1973) aptly remarked, 'Guardians of orthodoxy cannot rest when heresy is afoot. Who can stand idly by when traditional values are threatened and proven ways discarded?' But it is clear that both sides are equally guilty in this respect, as can be illustrated by the press publicity accorded the first publication (Bennett 1974) of the survey reported more fully in chapter 3. Even though a paragraph was inserted into the article containing a plea not to make political or educational capital out of the initial findings, newspapers of different political persuasions used the results to knock their own particular bogey men.

Indeed it would seem that the media have much to answer for in maintaining educational cleavages. Catch phrases, over-statement and misinterpretation undermine the value of educational debate and pander to the extremists on both sides. Issues such as these are unlikely to be resolved when considered in black-or-white, either/or terms. They are complex and require that evidence be presented and evaluated objectively.

Open education

It is interesting to note that the current controversy in the United States concerning the form that primary education should take there bears a strong resemblance to that in Britain in the post-Plowden era. Teaching methods in American elementary schools are generally more traditional in orientation compared with those in British schools and, as noted earlier, a movement is now afoot to implement a more open, informal approach by fanning the dying embers of progressive education into the bright new flame of 'open' education. Although some disciples of this new movement carefully attempt to delineate differences between open and progressive education, the following definition provided by Stephens (1974) demonstrates the amount of overlap.

Open education is an approach to education that is open to change, to new ideas, to curriculum, to scheduling, to use of space, to honest expressions of feeling between teacher and pupil and between pupil and pupil, and open to children's participation in significant decision-making in the classroom.

Open education is characterised by a classroom environment in which there is a minimum of teaching to the class as a whole, in which provision is made for children to pursue individual interests and to be actively involved with materials, and in which children are trusted to direct many aspects of their own learning.

It is, as Stephens admits, very similar to what is called informal or progressive education in Britain, and indeed the disciples of open education hold up practice in British primary schools as the ideal model. Featherstone, who is credited with being the first American to publicise British practice in the United States, wrote that 'by now the American interest in British primary schools is one distinct and powerful stream in a growing, turbulent movement for open informal schools' (1967). Concurrent with such comments has appeared a series of books extolling the virtues of British informal education (Rogers 1970; Silberman 1970; Rathbone 1971; Weber 1971; Barth 1972; Fisher 1972; Howe 1974): these reflect the 'droves of Americans' who have 'descended upon British schools in the last three years' sharing a romanticised vision of what they will see when they rush off to 'lighthouse' schools (Leese 1973). It is commonly believed, and stated, that one third of British schools follow the progressive model of teaching and more are moving towards it. American elementary teachers are now being urged to follow the doctrine, and workshops to aid them in its implementation are proliferating.

Prescription without evidence

Here too the innovation is being implemented, not on research evidence, but on faith. Silberman (1970) in his powerful denigration of formal methods could only muster two references to small scale studies and a story about an American visitor to Britain who asked an education officer if he had any statistics on student achievement that might permit comparison between informal and formal methods of teaching. In response the education officer opened a large, leather portfolio which contained samples of paintings, drawings, collages, embroideries, poems, stories and essays from informal schools. 'Here are the statistics' he replied. Stephens quotes the same two studies, perhaps indicating that the evidence reviewed in chapter 2 of this book is either irrelevant to the cause, or is insufficiently interesting to merit a thorough exposition.

It would seem clear that on both sides of the Atlantic innovation is being urged without research. This of course is not new in education, the common response being that educational decisions cannot afford to wait for years while careful trials are instituted and evaluated. Yet it is a strange logic which dictates that we *can* afford to implement changes in organisation and teaching which have unknown, and possibly deleterious, effects on the education of the nation's progeny.

What is also disturbing from the teachers' point of view is that they have been placed in a can't-win situation. They are criticised for mindlessly seizing on the new, the different, the flashy, the radical and the revolutionary, and for often distorting the ideas or practices from the original conception without recognising either the distortion or the assumptions violated by the distortion. Even the Plowden Report considered that teachers were weak on their theory, and other protagonists of progressive education admit that teachers did not take on these methods because of any deeply considered educational policy and practical foresight, but, like Kanga in *Winnie the Pooh*, 'did a good job without knowing it'. Teachers are in an educational no man's land, taking flak from left and right and being at the same time innovators and band-wagoners. Homage is paid to their autonomy at the same instant that they are being lambasted for failing to implement new practices which authors themselves admit are based on hunches, gut feelings and emotional responses.

The debate has centred around an either/or view of teaching – informal or formal, open or closed – but fortunately there is a growing body of educators who eschew such naïve arguments.

Hawkins (1966) writing in the context of the evaluation of discovery learning suggested that the issue should not be about better or worse ways of teaching. 'The notion that there is a single best way of teaching, across the universe of intellectual differences, of histories of preparation, of age, of teachers, is highly implausible.' Wittrock (1966), writing in the same volume, agreed, stating that 'individual differences may require several different approaches; with the variety of subject matter and students encountered in schools it is surely futile to expect one method of learning to be consistently superior or inferior to other plausible procedures.' In other words, to evaluate the effectiveness of differing teaching approaches requires data on their consequences for different types of pupil. The object of this study is to provide such evidence, and, in so doing, to answer Peters's plea for a 'down to earth, clear headed, empirical approach which takes due account, not only of general criteria, but of the differences in what is taught and the children to whom it is taught'.

2

Does teaching style make a difference?

The numerous books which have been written on progressive or open education give a false impression about the extent of research on teaching styles. This is perhaps not surprising since there does not appear to have been a systematic review of this research which has contained evidence from all the relevant sources – classroom observation, experimental studies, and comparative survey studies. Indeed a methodological rift appears to have developed between researchers wedded to different research methods, a rift similar to that noticed by Gage and Unruh (1967) among theorists of different persuasions 'who talk past each other in seemingly autistic disregard of what the others say'. This effect can be seen in recent reviews of research on teaching. Dunkin and Biddle (1974), although addressing their book to students of education who seek scientifically derived knowledge about instruction, restrict their review to systematic observation of teaching in classrooms. Similarly, Medley (1972), in tracing the history of research on teacher behaviour, deliberately excludes experimental evidence, arguing that experimental studies generally ignore differences in teacher behaviour other than those prescribed by the method adopted, or at best regard them as a source of error, and claimed that 'Such an approach is not likely to add to our understanding of teacher behaviour and its effects on pupils.'

Methodological myopia is not likely to provide a clear sighted view of the research terrain. So in the following exploration of research which has thrown light on the effects of teaching style on pupils' performance at primary level, no studies are excluded on methodological grounds. For ease of description these studies are considered under three headings: systematic observation, experimental studies and comparative survey studies.

These headings are not mutually exclusive, and therefore

require some explanation. The studies included under 'systematic observation' have all involved the observation of teacher and/or pupil behaviour, which is then recorded on some schedule containing behavioural categories.

The terms 'experimental' and 'comparative survey' are both used rather loosely to refer to studies on teaching in which classroom observation has not been undertaken. In experimental studies the researcher is ideally able to compare the performances of random or matched samples of pupils in relation to clearly specified differences in teaching behaviour. This is not true of comparative surveys. In these the researcher often chooses schools or teachers on the basis of subjective judgement, the criteria for which are rarely made explicit. The disadvantages of this type of approach are adumbrated later.

Systematic observation

Research on teaching has had a respectably long but, according to Gage (1972), a regrettably inglorious history. In sketching this history in the United States Medley (1972) discerned three phases. The first of these phases, extending from the beginning of the century to the early thirties, was concerned with factors involved in effective teaching. In the earlier studies students were requested to describe their most effective or best teachers. The culmination of these studies were lists of characteristics of 'good' teachers. This line of research was not particularly successful, possibly because the typical student has no more insight into the dynamics of teaching effectiveness than anyone else. As Medley put it, 'when asked to describe a good teacher he produces a mixture of trivia, banality, and common sense that adds nothing to what is already generally believed.' Researchers then turned to the opinions of educational experts, thereby producing other lists of 'good' teacher traits, which were even less useful than those produced by students.

A third approach was the use of rating scales, and by 1930 Barr and Emans had located 209 such instruments. Among the most popular areas rated were instruction, classroom management, and professional attitude. The limitations of this approach were that there was little consensus about the areas to be rated, or about the behaviours thought important in any given area. Probably the most serious drawback was that none of the studies included any measure of the effects of teachers on the pupils. Writers at that time were concerned about the lack of an 'adequate, concrete, objective, universal criterion for teaching ability', and suggested that this was the primary source of trouble for all who would measure teaching. Teacher ratings were regarded as amounting to arbitrary definitions of good teaching, which were subjective and usually vague.

The second phase identified by Medley was a dormant, interim period, lasting until the early 1960s. The foundations of a branch of educational research devoted to the analysis of teaching had been laid, and many of the blind alleys had been explored, 'but the explosion of interest did not take place for another twenty-five years'.

Hundreds of studies were carried out on the problem of teacher effectiveness in the period covered by these two phases, but they yielded disappointing results, and were usually lacking in educational or psychological meaning. Marsh and Wilder (1954), who reviewed the research that had been undertaken in the period 1900–52, concluded that 'no single, specific, observable teacher act has yet been found whose frequency or percentage of occurrence has invariably and significantly correlated with student achievement.' The equivocality of research findings was further demonstrated by Anderson (1959) who, in considering thirty-two studies, reported that eleven supported superior learning in learner centred classes, eight in teacher centred classes, and thirteen showed no difference. Medley and Mitzel (1963) argued that much work on teacher effectiveness must be discarded as irrelevant because it lacked criteria and objective measures, and in the same volume Gage (1963) and Wallen and Travers (1963) both concluded that change in pupils seemed largely unaffected by style of teaching. In other words there was little evidence that teaching methods made any difference (cf. Baldwin 1965, Stephens 1967).

Wallen and Travers concluded more optimistically that the 'era of research comparing one teaching method with another is coming to a close', but they could not have been wider of the mark. Instead refinements were sought both in modes of data-gathering and in the conceptualisation of the variables which should be considered. Researchers began to move away from rating scales which usually require relatively subjective estimates of teacher characteristics, towards more objective observation schedules. These are classified as 'low inference' measures because they focus upon specific, objectively describable behaviours such as 'teacher asks for pupil ideas' or 'teacher criticises/praises pupil'. These behaviours are recorded as frequency counts. The categories used by Flanders (1970) provide an example (table 2.1). With this schedule observations are taken every three seconds and a tally recorded in the appropriate category. Brandt (1972) provides a useful introduction to this area.

This new approach represents the third phase outlined by Medley, the stimulus for which he attributes to Anderson (1939) and Jayne (1945). He sees three important characteristics of such approaches. Firstly, they measure meaningful and potentially important behaviour patterns or traits; secondly, they retain the objectivity and reliability of the original items on which they are based; and thirdly, since the dimensions are measured in terms of specific behaviours they are much more useful in helping the teacher to effect change in his behaviour should he wish to do so.

The conceptualisation of the sets of variables to be included in the study of teaching has led to the broad acceptance of a model initially proposed by Mitzel (1957). Figure 2.1 presents an adaptation of this model by Dunkin and Biddle (1974).

Here the classroom is symbolised by a rectangle. To the left of this are three sets of variables that are thought to influence classroom events or processes; those associated with the teacher, the pupils, and the contexts of community, school and classroom. To the right are the hypothesised products of education. The arrows represent sources of hypotheses rather than symbols of invariant truth.

There are thirteen classes of variables suggested in the figure, but for the sake of convenience, and given the present state of research, these are reduced to four larger classes, presage, context, process and product. Presage variables relate to the characteristics of teachers, their experiences, their cognitive and affective properties. Context variables as used by Dunkin and Biddle relate to the conditions to which the teacher has to adjust, the characteristics of the school, classroom and pupils. Process

Teacher talk	Response	1 *Accepts feeling* Accepts and clarifies attitude or feeling tone of a pupil in a non-threatening manner. Feelings may be positive or negative. Predicting and recalling feelings are included. 2 *Praises or encourages* Praises or encourages pupil action or behaviour. Jokes that release tension, but not at the expense of another individual; nodding head, or saying 'Um hm?' or 'Go on' are included. 3 *Accepts or uses ideas of pupils* Clarifying, building, or developing ideas suggested by a pupil. Teacher extensions of pupil ideas are included but as the teacher brings more of his own ideas into play, shift to category five.
		4 *Asks questions* Asking a question about content or procedure, based on teacher ideas with the intent that a pupil will answer.
	Initiation	5 *Lecturing* Giving facts or opinions about content or procedures; expressing his own ideas, giving his own explanation, or citing an authority other than a pupil. 6 *Giving directions* Directions, commands, or orders with which a pupil is expected to comply. 7 *Criticising or justifying authority* Statements intended to change pupil behaviour from non-acceptable to acceptable pattern; bawling someone out; stating why the teacher is doing what he is doing; extreme self-reference.
Pupil talk	Response	8 *Pupil-talk-response* Talk by pupils in response to teacher. Teacher initiates the contact or solicits pupil statement or structures the situation. Freedom to express own ideas is limited.
	Initiation	9 *Pupil-talk-initiation* Talk by pupils which they initiate. Expressing own ideas; initiating a new topic; freedom to develop opinions and a line of thought, like asking thoughtful questions; going beyond the existing structure.
Silence		10 *Silence or confusion* Pauses, short periods of silence and periods of confusion in which communication cannot be understood by the observer.

Table 2.1 *Category descriptions used by Flanders in interaction analysis* (1970, p. 34)

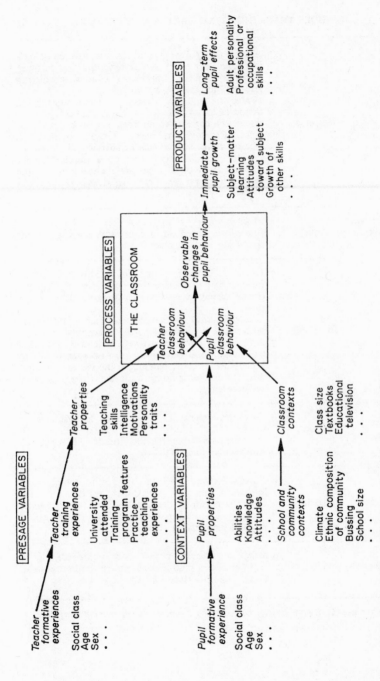

Figure 2.1 A model for the study of classroom teaching

variables concern the actual activities of classroom teaching, teacher and pupil behaviour and their interaction and the type of classroom climate engendered. Finally, product variables concern the outcomes of teaching, the changes that occur in pupils as a result of their involvement in classroom activities. The term 'pupil growth' or 'pupil change' can relate to both cognitive and affective characteristics.

Studies have tended to be categorised in terms of these four larger classes. Thus a study of the relationship between teacher personality and teacher classroom behaviour is called a presage-process study, whereas a study relating classroom behaviour and change in pupil attainment is termed process-product.

Mitzel argued that the best hope of improving research on teaching lay in the study of process variables, and this appears to have been largely accepted by most researchers in this area. So too has the premise that measures of pupil growth are the ultimate criteria for research on teaching effects (Rosenshine and Furst 1973).

Since the introduction of research based on this model some reviews of research have tended to be slightly more optimistic about the possibility of isolating the factors involved in teacher effectiveness (Flanders and Simon 1969; Rosenshine 1970, 1971; Gage 1972). Rosenshine has provided the most thorough review of studies which have related teacher behaviours and characteristics to pupil growth. The most consistent results have emanated from the general 'indirectness' measure of Flanders. An indirect teacher in Flanders's scheme is one who accepts feeling, praises and encourages, and uses pupils' ideas. By contrast the direct teacher is one who tends to lecture, give directions, and criticise. Flanders claims that 'the percentage of teacher statements that made use of ideas and opinions previously expressed by pupils is directly related to average class scores on attitude scales of teacher attractiveness and liking the class, as well as to average achievement scores adjusted for initial ability' (Flanders and Simon 1969). Other characteristics which have turned out to be consistently related to pupil gain have been teacher warmth, enthusiasm and, in a negative direction, teacher criticism. Rosenshine and Furst (1973) and Dunkin and Biddle (1974) have provided the latest reviews of such studies.

The problem with reviews of this kind is that all studies are considered together, irrespective of the age and sex of the samples, the type of content covered, and the product measures used, the implicit assumption being that there is one best way of teaching everything to everybody. What follows is therefore a résumé of research restricted to the context of this investigation – process-product studies at primary level. All the studies mentioned in this résumé were carried out in the United States, which reflects the greater emphasis on this type of research in that country.

The early work of Anderson was restricted to infant schools but research carried out by Flanders is based heavily upon Anderson's theorising. In Flanders's earlier studies classrooms were chosen in which pupils had more favourable or less favourable attitudes towards the classroom, and observational data were then collected. These data were related to both attitude and achievement measures. Typical results indicated that positive relationships existed between teacher indirectness, pupil achievement growth, and more positive attitudes. However the relationships were variable and not always significant as Rosenshine (1971) points out in his critical review.

A number of other investigators have used the Flanders system and are reviewed in Flanders (1970). La Shier and Westmeyer (1967) related teacher behaviour to pupil achievement gain and attitudes in a unit of the Biological Science Curriculum Study. Both were found to be positively related to teacher indirectness. Furst (1967), reworking data collected by Bellack and others (1966), also found a composite variable of indirect teacher behaviour related positively to pupil achievement. Powell (1968) and Weber (1968) analysed different growth measures from pupils in the same classrooms. Nine teachers whose pupils had remained with them through grades one to three (pupils of six to eight years old) were observed, together with the teachers to whom the pupils moved for grade four. The nine teachers of grades one to three were classified as direct or indirect, and pupil differences in achievement and creativity were examined. Powell found that indirect teaching was associated with higher scores for arithmetic and a higher composite achievement measure, but not with a higher score for reading. Weber found significantly higher scores on reveral verbal creativity measures for pupils who had

had indirect teachers in grades one to three. Neither investigator found differences associated with teaching style in grade four when the effect of the first three years was statistically controlled.

This would seem to indicate that the relationship between teacher behaviour and pupil growth could vary by grade level, and there is other evidence to support this argument. In Flanders's research, studies using upper grade students tend to show a positive relationship between teacher sustained acceptance of pupil ideas and pupil cognitive growth, but in a second grade sample a negative relationship was found. Similarly, Wallen (1966) found differences in relationship at first and third grade.

There are also indications that there may be an interaction between teaching style and ability levels. Schantz (1963) found that high ability pupils exhibited greater growth under indirect than under direct teaching, while there was no difference in the effect of teaching style for low ability pupils. Calvin, Hoffman and Harden (1957) also found that permissive teaching led to greater growth for high I.Q. pupils, but handicapped subjects with average I.Q.

The Observation Schedule and Record (OScAR) developed by Medley and Mitzel (1958) has also been used to assess the relationship of teaching style and pupil growth. In one study the emotional climate index of OScAR related only modestly to growth in reading (Medley and Mitzel 1959). Using a modified OScAR Harris and Serwer (1966) and Harris and others (1968) gained somewhat contradictory results from their sample of disadvantaged children. In the first study positive but non-significant relationships were found between teacher criticism (negative motivation) and pupil growth in spelling, and between teacher control and growth in reading. In the second study a negative relationship was found between teacher criticism and reading.

Thompson and Bowers (1968) used a later version of the instrument to relate teaching style and growth in creative abilities. They found that a higher frequency of teacher talk was related to greater growth in non-verbal creativity on the part of the children, and that a more direct teaching style together with average verbal output was associated with greater total creativity growth. Wodtke and Wallen (1965) also investigated differences in creative growth with nineteen high and low controlling teachers in grades two to five. Greater verbal creative growth was found in pupils with low control teachers, and greater non-verbal growth with high control teachers. Turner and Denny (1969) found a positive relationship between child centred (as against subject centred) teaching and gain in pupil creativity scores, although with a different observational instrument.

Few studies at the elementary level have used more than one observational instrument, or more than one or two cognitive and affective measures. Thus the study by Soar (1966) is of particular interest and relevance, and is described in greater detail.

The sample was fifty-seven teachers of grades three to six (age range 9–12) in four 'unusually good', high morale, upper middle class schools. The Flanders instrument was used in addition to the South Carolina Observation Record (SCOR). Pupil measures included tests of vocabulary, reading, arithmetic and creativity, together with tests of anxiety, dependence, motivation and social relations. Classes were observed over two years.

In reporting the results on cognitive growth, Soar identified two factors, one representing teacher control, and the other emotional climate. In relating pupil gain in vocabulary, reading and creativity to those two factors he found that greater gain in vocabulary was associated with indirect teacher control and a low climate of hostility. On reading and creativity the findings were not as clear cut but gains in both appeared to be related to indirect control.

Soar hypothesised relationships (which would be non-linear: see below) between indirect teacher behaviour and these measures as follows: greater gain in creativity should occur in classrooms where teacher behaviour was most indirect; greater gains in vocabulary should occur in classrooms where teachers were somewhat less indirect; and greater reading gains should occur in classrooms where teachers were even less indirect. The results supported this.

On this evidence Soar (1972) postulated the general principle that the more complex or abstract the pupil gain measure (i.e. creativity is a more complex and abstract activity than reading), the more indirect the teacher behaviour which is associated with most growth. He also suggested that there is an upper limit to the degree of indirectness which is supportive of a particular kind of achievement growth, and that beyond that point less growth occurs. Thus the two aspects of the general principle are, first, that the relation of academic progress to differing degrees of classroom control is likely to be non-linear, i.e. to have an optimal level intermediate between 'most' and 'least', neither extreme being best; and second, that the relationships and optimal levels are likely to vary, depending on the complexity and abstractness of the attainment measure.

Soar thus postulated that in a representative sample the relationship between teacher indirectness and pupil progress in attainment areas of different complexity will appear as in figure 2.2. On the basis of this theory it could be hypothesised that informal classrooms would foster greater gains in creativity, whereas formal teaching would create greater gains in reading.

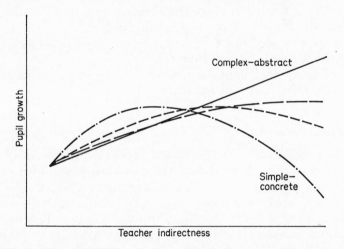

Figure 2.2 *Hypothetical relation between pupil growth and teacher indirectness across a broad range*

This seems to be a useful avenue for further research although the theoretical rationale for ranking school subjects on the complex-concrete dimension appears to be the weak link.

Soar also found an interaction between teaching approach and achievement gain dependent upon the level of stress engendered by each teaching approach. He maintained that greatest stress is evident in classrooms where there is direct control and a non-supportive climate, whereas greatest growth in vocabulary was associated with minimum stress, and greatest growth in reading with moderate levels of stress. He concluded that pupils differing in anxiety level will differ as to which teaching style is most beneficial for them in terms of academic progress.

Summary
The evidence from observational studies at the elementary level can be summarised as follows.

1 Although the evidence is equivocal it would appear that indirect (and/or less hostile) teacher behaviours are generally more conducive to pupil growth on most achievement measures.

2 There is a possibility that these relationships may vary or be non-linear, depending upon (i) the task complexity of the achievement measure, (ii) grade level and (iii) level of ability of pupils.

3 There is evidence that these relationships may be mediated by the anxiety level of the pupil.

4 Indirect teaching behaviours appear to generate more positive attitudes to school and schoolwork.

Experimental studies

To disregard such studies is to disregard many investigations relating teaching method to educational outcomes, since a number of experiments have compared progressive or activity schools with their traditional counterparts. The most extensive of these was conducted under the auspices of the American Progressive Education Association in the period 1933–9, and is commonly known as the 'Eight Year Study': though this study concentrated on students in secondary and tertiary education. Wallen and Travers (1963) summarised experimental research at primary level as follows:

In the early grades, students in the progressive curriculum tend to perform somewhat below expectation in reading and arithmetic but overcome their inferiority by sixth grade; they tend to be average or somewhat superior throughout their school years in achievement areas involving language usage; when moving up to junior high school, they suffer no handicap in dealing with a more traditional curriculum; when compared on tests designed to measure work skills, organising ability, ability to interpret information, and civic beliefs, they score higher but often not significantly so; they tend to be better informed on current affairs, and they tend to be rated higher by school teachers and independent observers on such dimensions as initiative, work spirit and critical thinking. In summary, the findings indicate no important differences in terms of subject matter mastery and a superiority of the progressive students in terms of the characteristics which the progressive school seeks to develop.

More recent experimental research at the elementary level has taken achievement in arithmetic as the dependent variable. The results have been equivocal, as the following studies demonstrate. Sax and Ottina (1958) set out to assess the truth of the statement that 'Practice or drill on the fundamental phases of arithmetic is essential if the needs of children are to be met. The saving of time and energy, to say nothing of the confidence generated, which automatic mastery of essential arithmetic affords is sufficient verification of the principle.' They gave tests of arithmetic at the end of grades three, four, five, six and seven to pupils in progressive and conventional schools. At third and fourth grade, pupils in conventional schools made significantly higher scores on standard computation, but not at fifth, sixth and seventh grade. These results would seem to support the earlier studies in their claim that no differences are discernible beyond sixth grade.

Guggenheim (1961) matched 195 pupils at the beginning of third grade and re-tested after one year using a test of mathematical concepts. Classrooms were classified as dominative, where the approach was teacher centred, and integrative, where teacher–pupil relationships were warm. The sample was split into three levels of mathematics achievement, but no differences were found at any level.

Kieren (1968), reviewing research on activity learning and mathematics performance reported between 1964 and 1968, concluded that the studies did little to solve the theoretical conflict, the results being mixed, and the methodologies often poorly defined.

In a recent tightly controlled experiment Olander and Robertson (1973) studied the effect of teaching mathematics by discovery and expository methods at fourth grade level. 190 pupils in seven classes were given the discovery treatment, and 184 pupils in nine classes were given the expository treatment. All teachers used the same textbook, but those adopting discovery methods used concrete objects, models and representative materials to facilitate discovery, whereas the teachers giving the expository treatment used the text as the prime source of ideas. Pupils were tested for arithmetic computation, concepts and applications. It was found that pupils given the expository treatment scored slightly better in computation and application, and pupils given the discovery treatment scored better on concepts. Pupil attitudes to mathematics were also tested, and these were found to improve significantly in the discovery treatment.

Further analyses indicated that pupils who initially scored low on computation and application did better in the expository treatment, whereas pupils who had scored highly on these aspects performed better in the discovery treatment. This effect was reversed for arithmetic concepts.

Another set of experimental studies has attempted to assess the interaction between pupil personality and teaching styles (Bracht and Glass 1968; Cronbach and Snow 1969; Bracht 1970; Berliner and Cahen 1973; Gustafsson 1974). So far results have generally been disappointing, although Trown (1973), who recently reviewed this evidence, suggests that at primary level anxious children perform better in arithmetic with a more supportive structure whereas non-anxious children perform much better in an exploratory structure (cf. Leith and Bossett 1967). This effect has also been reported by Grimes and Allinsmith (1961). Although they were particularly interested in reading achievement, a range of measures including tests of language, spelling and arithmetic were administered to a random sample of third grade children in structured and unstructured teaching situations. In relating scores on these measures to compulsivity and anxiety they found that highly compulsive pupils in structured settings scored significantly higher marks than their counterparts in unstructured settings. Highly compulsive pupils performed better than less compulsive pupils in structured settings, but no difference was apparent in unstructured settings. This effect was similar for anxiety. Highly anxious pupils in unstructured settings performed significantly worse than those in structured settings. Also, whilst highly anxious pupils achieved significantly less in unstructured classes than low anxious pupils, they appeared to perform at least as well as the average in structured classes, and perceived unabated threat in the unstructured, ambiguous situations.

Although Trown found little evidence of interactions between teaching method and extroversion there is evidence to indicate that extroverts perform better in unstructured discovery treatment and introverts in highly structured ones. Such interactions are thought to be one reason why comparisons between teaching methods in the past have produced results indicating no difference. 'It is not that the different methods are interchangeable – rather that each is successful and unsuccessful with different kinds of pupils' (Leith 1972). Trown therefore concluded that complex effects in relation to anxiety and extroversion suggest that not only is a total specification of learning situations necessary to understanding, but analysis of other dimensions of pupil personality and ability is also necessary for full insight. In effect she reiterates the claim made by Cronbach and Snow (1969) that there is considerable reason to think that the student's personality does effect his response to the classroom and that this ought to be researched.

Comparative survey studies

Experiments on other subject areas at elementary level appear to be lacking, although evidence is available from studies which have chosen schools or classrooms for comparison based on 'expert' opinion, or reputation. In general these studies tend to be unsatisfactory and take the following form: choose the schools, classes or teachers 'by repute'; administer tests on one occasion; from resultant data make inferences about the effect of the schools, classes or teachers. Pupil growth is not assessed.

Typical of this approach is the study by Minuchin and others (1969), which investigated differences in four American middle-class urban schools varying on a modern–traditional dimension. The sample was 105 nine- and ten-year-old boys and girls who were tested on a range of cognitive and affective measures. The cognitive tests included verbal reasoning and problem solving skills. On these the pupils in the modern schools performed less well than their counterparts in traditional schools. Imaginative (divergent) thinking tests were included but produced no differences. Role-playing techniques were also used to assess imaginative functioning, but again no stable group differences emerged.

On the affective side, analyses indicated that there were more rational objective attitudes to authority in the modern schools, and more fearfulness and conformity in the traditional schools. Few differences were found in their assessments of pupil self concept.

Sex differences were noted whereby girls were more comfortable and identified with the school more in the traditional schools, whereas boys were more restless and negative. In the modern schools both boys and girls identified with school and enjoyed it. The authors also noted that in the traditional schools impulsive children floundered, and in the modern schools children failed who needed structure.

British studies of a similar type have compared progressive and traditional schools. Richards and Bolton (1971) studied arithmetic performance in three primary schools designated traditional, mixed and modern, based on type of arithmetic teaching. They found that pupils in the traditional school performed better on standardised tests than did the pupils in the modern school, but that the best performance came from the school using mixed methods.

Haddon and Lytton (1968) gave divergent thinking tests to pupils in primary schools designated formal or informal by college of education lecturers. The pupils in informal schools gained significantly higher scores than those in formal schools, and on this basis it was suggested that informal schools provide an environment which is more conducive to the development of divergent abilities. In another study of this type Lovell (1963) found no difference between the reading attainments of children attending formal and informal schools, whereas Gardner (1966) did, although this latter study is unsatisfactory in many respects.

A major study on British primary schools also throws some light on this area (Barker Lunn 1970). Although primarily concerned with the effects of streaming, teacher types were created by grouping together teachers who had similar attitudes, who taught in schools of similar organisation and who taught the same type of lessons. Two types were extracted from the analysis, one approximating to the progressive teacher (type 1), and the other to the traditional teacher (type 2). The type 1 teacher was more permissive, more tolerant of noise, used more progressive lessons and had an unfavourable attitude towards corporal punishment. The type 2 teacher had the opposite characteristics. Type of teacher was then related to pupil change in divergent thinking and imaginative story scores. Over all, pupils with a type 1 teacher tended to show an improvement in these areas, whereas those with a type 2 teacher did not. Although there were no significant differences in terms of the imaginative story, type 1 teachers were associated with a greater number of high scorers on both divergent thinking tests and imaginative stories.

Pupil gain on other achievement measures, including English and arithmetic, was also related to teacher type, but few differences emerged. One of the reasons put forward to explain this was that the categories of teacher used were too gross, a point taken up again in the critique at the end of this chapter.

Summary
A comparison of the results gained from experimental and comparative survey research with the four summary points derived from the review of observation studies indicates a degree of agreement, particularly in relation to the interactive effect of pupil personality. The four summary points were:

1 Indirect (and/or less hostile) teacher behaviours are generally more conducive to pupil growth on most achievement measures.

This receives little support. Results have been mixed, and few significant differences recorded. However there would seem to be some support for the positive relationship between progressive approaches and pupil growth in the creativity area.

2 There is a possibility that these relationships may vary or be non-linear depending upon (i) the task complexity of the achievement measure, (ii) grade level and (iii) level of ability of pupils.

There would seem to be some support for (i) from the Olander and Robertson study if the assumption that arithmetic concepts constitute a more complex task than arithmetic computation is accepted. Greater gain in concepts was achieved under the discovery treatment. Some support for a non-linear relationship could also be claimed from the Richards and Bolton study where the mixed school produced the best results in arithmetic performance.

Differences in grade level were commented upon by both Wallen and Travers, and Sax and Ottina. Although few experiments considered ability level there is again some evidence from the Olander and Robertson study. In addition, sex of pupil was put forward as a mediating influence by Minuchin.

3 There is evidence that these relationships may be mediated by the anxiety level of the pupil.

This receives the greatest support. The evidence extends this to include not only anxiety, but compulsivity and extroversion. These results lend support to Cronbach's (1966) assertions concerning the interaction of pupil characteristics and teaching approach. He thought that 'the interesting variables may have more to do with personality than with ability; I am tempted by the notion that pupils who are negativistic may blossom under discovery training, whereas pupils who are anxiously dependent may be paralysed by demands for self reliance.' He therefore argued that 'we have to explore a five-fold interaction – subject matter, with type of instruction, with timing of instruction, with type of pupil, with outcome.'

4 Indirect teaching behaviours appear to generate more positive attitudes to school and schoolwork.

Little research appears to have been carried out relating motivation to teaching approach, although there is some support from the earlier studies reviewed by Wallen and Travers.

CRITIQUE

Reviews of literature have, over the years, veered erratically between optimism and pessimism about the possibility of isolating the factors involved in differential pupil progress, and before the fairly optimistic conclusions of the last sections can be accepted they must be judged in the light of the conceptual, methodological and statistical limitations of the studies involved.

Perhaps the greatest problem in this area is that of definition of terms. In the introduction it will have been noted that such terms as 'informal', 'progressive', 'discovery', 'permissive', 'egalitarian' and 'open' were used synonymously, and often emotively. This diversity accurately reflects the literature. The acute problem of ambiguous operational definitions was highlighted by Travers (1971) who contended that it is in this area that

we have a long tradition of using very sloppy and hazy variables such as traditional and progressive, or pupil-centred and teacher-centred, or authoritarian and democratic. All of these have been 'defined' in terms of general categories of behaviour, but since the limits of the categories are never specified the concepts remain obscure.

The three dichotomies mentioned by Travers represent, to paraphrase Flanders (1965), but a short stroll in the conceptual garden; an overnight hike could extend the list indefinitely.

These problems are confounded by the fact that the same terms are used to describe different aspects of the classroom situation, and different terms used to refer to essentially the same aspects. In commenting on this confusion Herbert (1967) concluded that the term 'teaching method' had no stable meaning, and that descriptions of particular methods are too vague or inconsistent to permit an observer to distinguish them in practice.

Equally problematic is the fact that the general terms used can often mean all things to all men. Kendler (1966) for example branded 'discovery' a nine letter dirty word that should be abolished, and on the same theme Stones (1973) has argued that 'the use of the word to refer to a vague and undifferentiated set of concepts in a general undifferentiated way causes several problems. Spurious consensus is inevitable if the one word means all (and different) things to different people.' It would therefore seem necessary to break down such concepts into their constituent elements since there is a possibility that they may be composed of independent factors. Soar (1967) has demonstrated this with the term 'permissive'. He reasoned that recent research had indicated that the term could involve two dimensions – the emotional climate of the classroom, and the degree of closeness of control exercised by the teacher. Teachers could show warmth towards their pupils whilst also exercising a high degree of control. In addition there may be two subdivisions of control – tightness of control in the teacher's verbal interaction with the pupils, and control of physical movement. Emotional climate may also be subdivided, one facet being the expression of emotion by the teacher and the other being the expression of emotion by the pupils. Siegel and Siegel (1967) have been similarly critical of the grossness of the definition of teaching method in experimental studies, and claim that this has confounded results.

Definitions of the independent variables in comparative survey studies are even more nebulous. Since these definitions are commonly based on subjective judgements, the criteria underlying which are rarely made explicit, generalisations and replications are impossible.

A similar problem of a different type is apparent in the delineation of teacher types from data derived from category systems where there is a tendency to treat a teacher characteristic as a fixed attribute. The direct–indirect dimension of Flanders illustrates this point. Investigators who have used this system, or a derivative of it, divide their teacher sample into direct or indirect on the basis of their observations in the classroom. However, since representative samples in classroom research are rare, the dividing line between direct and indirect is different in every study. This could mean that the same teacher could be categorised as direct in one study and indirect in another, depending on the characteristics of the remainder of the sample he happens to be in. In effect this would count against generalising results outside the particular sample used. The summary points derived from the review of observational research must therefore be set against these criticisms.

The sampling problem is particularly acute in this respect since generalisations from what have been essentially 'opportunity' samples are impossible, and the problem is exacerbated by the fact that no data are available on how teachers teach in the population at large. The reasons why samples have been small and opportunist are not difficult to locate, and have been spelled out by Adams (1972): 'the inherent complexity of the classroom setting, and the consequent cost of researching it, have ensured that samples are small, that representativeness is rare and that random samples are almost never achieved.' Dunkin and Biddle (1974) are more definite, stating that they have located *no* study which used a random sample.

Poor sampling of teachers is paralleled by poor sampling of classroom events. Observation schedules typically concentrate on a narrow range of teacher and pupil behaviour, and very few investigators use more than one schedule. Rosenshine and Furst (1973) in their review indicate that most studies have concentrated on affective aspects of classroom life, and complain that 'in practice the development of instruments for the analysis of teaching has come to mean no more than a description of some aspects of instruction along with an interpretation which objectifies the author's bias.' They continue: 'the proliferation of observational systems without validation ... has led to the current chaos which is a pretense of research.'

A major aspect of the validity of such instruments relates to their coverage of the range of classroom events. 'The current emphasis on observational studies has produced a proliferation of observational systems and frequency counts of the *minutiae* of teacher and student behaviour in their daily situations' (Nuthall and Snook 1973). Criticisms of the content coverage include the fact that they disregard the materials being read, the assignments students write, the teachers' use of written and oral material, and the physical features of the room such as seating arrangements and lighting (Rosenshine and Furst 1973).

Research on teaching in natural settings has to date tended to be chaotic, unorganised and self serving (Rosenshine and Furst 1973), and one of the basic reasons for this appears to be that too many studies have been based on 'dust-bowl empiricism' – studies with no theoretical rationale. 'It must be obvious to the critical reader that what is missing from many of the reported studies is the sense of direction and controlled orderliness which can only be provided by adequate theory' (Nuthall 1968). This author then goes on to express the opinion that stretching old psychological theories is of little value. What is required is the creation of new theory 'which arises directly from the natural grain and detail of the behaviour it is supposed to explain'. This argument is akin to the grounded theory approach espoused by Glaser and Strauss (1967). Unfortunately classroom researchers have, until now, been content merely to describe rather than use their descriptions in the development of mini-models (cf. Snow 1973). Until more model-development is carried out we are left in a position akin to that of the prospector whose theory is precise enough to indicate that some locations are more likely places to dig than others, but not accurate enough to pinpoint the nuggets – we are still sifting the gravel, with occasional flecks of gold (Soar 1967).

It would therefore appear that investigators have commonly observed a narrow range of the behaviour of a small and unrepresentative sample of teachers drawn from a population of unknown parameters, and have categorised them according to some global, ill-defined dichotomy, unrelated to any theoretical perspective.

Another factor which has led to inconsistency of results is that most investigators appear to have assumed that the effect of the teaching styles is constant for all types of pupils. In other words the studies have been designed to assess the question 'Is teaching style A better than teaching style B?' The review of studies on pupil growth at primary level indicates that the effect is not constant. Studies of this type could therefore be masking interesting interactive effects because of their failure to differentiate types of pupils. Studies in future should therefore be designed to answer the added question 'Do teaching styles interact with pupil characteristics to produce differential outcomes?'

It was these sorts of basic questions that the present study was designed to answer. More specifically these were: Do differences in teaching style differentially affect the cognitive and emotional development of pupils? Do certain types of pupil perform better under certain types of teaching style?

RESEARCH DESIGN

In creating the most appropriate and effective research design to answer these questions, it was obviously necessary that a clearer and more sophisticated methodological and conceptual treatment be given to a number of points thrown up by the critique above.

(i) Following Soar, the teaching styles described by single, general terms should first be broken down into their constituent behaviours, so that a clear definition of terms becomes possible.

(ii) Following Rosenshine and Furst, the range of teacher behaviours contained within the definition of style should be widened to increase the validity of the description.

(iii) Misleadingly simple descriptions in the form of dichotomies should be abandoned in favour of a multidimensional approach.

Stake (1970) is in no doubt about what is needed: 'some easy to administer, easy to understand, not very controversial, but valid, method of describing teaching'. Something is needed 'that appeals to the clinical experience of the teacher and that suits the technical sophistication of administrators and laymen'. Common prose is not the answer. There is some general understanding when one says 'lecture' or 'authoritarian style' or 'discovery method', but also misunderstanding. He therefore recommends multidimensional typologies of teaching styles but notes that 'educators are offended by typologies that . . . might lead to some greater understanding of what is happening in the classroom. To call a Professor "Type III" or even "Type 3-16-4-0-9" is to invite being spat on. Yet the need for description, classification and even over-simplification is apparent.'

A multidimensional analysis is also called for in delineating pupil types. Soar (1972) has noted that growing evidence for the existence of complex interactions between classroom behaviour, the learning task and pupil characteristics point strongly to the need for more subtle, complex and extensive research on classroom learning. But this brings with it attendant conceptual issues. What has to be taken into account if a reasonably full and representative sample of pupil characteristics is required? Sells (1963) for example estimated that more than one hundred different variables would have to be accommodated if a full and sufficient description of human behaviour were to be achieved.

(iv) Attempts should be made to validate the description of teaching styles, or in other words to assess whether the empirically derived styles relate to the realities of the classroom.

(v) A more sophisticated sampling design is required which allows for the description of population parameters of teaching styles, and – as important – allows a representative sample of teachers to be selected.

(vi) The time interval in observational and experimental studies has typically been short, yet educational recommendations seek to optimise students' growth over a long time-span. Carroll (1963) and Cronbach (1966) have urged that studies of instruction should be continued over a substantial time-span. This time span should be of sufficient duration to enable the pupil to be familiar with the style of instruction. 'Educational policy cannot be based on what the pupil does in his first encounter with an instructional style' (Cronbach and Snow 1969). Following this, studies should have a long time base.

(vii) The study should be theoretically based if possible and, if not, should take note of the locations of the 'flecks of gold' previously found.

The research design of the study was created with these seven critical points in mind, and was made up of the following stages:

1 Break down the terms 'progressive' and 'traditional' into their constituent elements via a review of relevant literature and interviews with primary school teachers. Operationalise the elements in terms of questionnaire items so that they can be measured objectively.

2 After the questionnaire has been designed and piloted administer it to a large and representative sample of teachers.

3 Use cluster analysis to create a typology of teaching styles by grouping together teachers who responded to the questionnaire items similarly.

4 Validate the typology by independent ratings based on classroom observation and perception of pupils.

5 Select a representative sample of teachers from each teaching type by choosing those teachers who most closely reflect the central profile of each type.

6 Shift from a survey to a quasi-experimental research design by following through one school year the pupils of the teacher samples. Pre-test pupils on entry using a wide range of cognitive and affective instruments, and post-test prior to exit.

7 To assess the relationship between pupil personality and

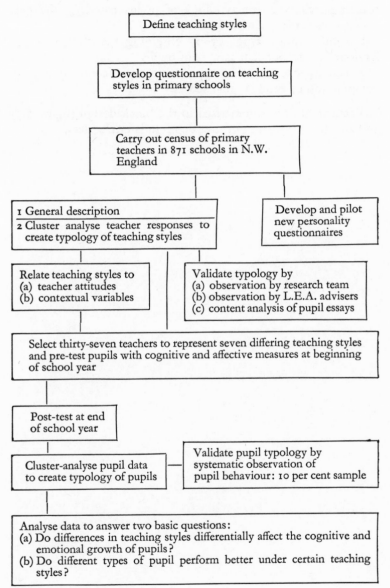

Figure 2.3 *Simplified research design*

teaching style, create a typology of pupils based on the personality tests, using cluster analysis.

8 Validate pupil typology by observing the classroom behaviour of a 10 per cent sample of pupils.

9 Test hypotheses using appropriate statistical analyses, e.g. computation of residual gain scores.

These stages are summarised in the block design (figure 2.3) and are all dealt with in greater depth in later chapters.

3

A typology of teaching styles

The first task of the study was to break down the global terms 'progressive' and 'traditional' into their constituent elements before translating these elements into questionnaire items. One obvious approach was to review the many alternative conceptions of the teaching process which abound in the philosophical and psychological literature related to education. This was the first step taken, and included an examination of the theoretical and philosophical underpinnings of, to use Sherman's (1970) labels, the Platonic, instrumental approach versus the Rousseauian, naturalistic alternative; and a review of the differing psychological interpretations of the learning process, notably the behaviourist and cognitive theories, and of disputes such as that between Bruner (1961) and Ausubel (1963) concerning student motivation and creative growth. It also included an examination of the various educational reports, notably Hadow (1931) and Plowden (1967), both of which grounded their prescriptions on similar literature.

A purely theoretical breakdown was deemed insufficient, particularly since it would appear that teachers take little cognisance of such literature in determining their natural teaching style. This fact was noted in the Plowden report which considered that it was rare to find teachers who had given much time to the study of educational theory, even in their college of education days. It was therefore decided to complement the theoretical review with interviews with primary school teachers who, in the subjective opinion of the author, represented the range of teaching styles under consideration. Head and class teachers from twelve schools were interviewed to ascertain what teaching behaviours they considered differentiated progressive and traditional styles.

Progressive	Traditional
1 Integrated subject matter	1 Separate subject matter
2 Teacher as guide to educational experiences	2 Teacher as distributor of knowledge
3 Active pupil role	3 Passive pupil role
4 Pupils participate in curriculum planning	4 Pupils have no say in curriculum planning
5 Learning predominantly by discovery techniques	5 Accent on memory, practice and rote
6 External rewards and punishments not necessary, i.e. intrinsic motivation	6 External rewards used, e.g. grades, i.e. extrinsic motivation
7 Not too concerned with conventional academic standards	7 Concerned with academic standards
8 Little testing	8 Regular testing
9 Accent on cooperative group work	9 Accent on competition
10 Teaching not confined to classroom base	10 Teaching confined to classroom base
11 Accent on creative expression	11 Little emphasis on creative expression

Table 3.1 *Characteristics of progressive and traditional teachers*

From these diverse sources eleven basic differentiating elements were isolated and are shown in table 3.1. The elements were translated into classroom behaviours and then into questionnaire items. The final version of the questionnaire covered six major areas:

1 *Classroom management and organisation:* extent of freedom of movement and talk in the classroom, seating arrangements adopted

2 *Teacher control and sanctions:* degree of disciplinary rather than physical control

3 *Curriculum content and planning:* allocation of teaching time, extent of timetabling and homework, degree of pupil choice

4 *Instructional strategies:* type of teaching approach

5 *Motivational techniques:* whether intrinsic or extrinsic motivation is stressed

6 *Assessment procedures:* type and quantity of evaluation of pupil work

Two pilot studies were carried out to make possible the reduction and modification of ambiguous items. The final form of the questionnaire contained twenty-eight items although a number were in multiple form. Question 28 for example required a breakdown of the time spent on every aspect of the syllabus in the last full week prior to completing the questionnaire. Similarly question 16 required the teachers to indicate the time spent on five basic pedagogical approaches. The questionnaire in its final form was included as a separate section of a larger questionnaire which also contained sections on the teacher, class and classroom and on teacher opinions about educational issues. The whole of this questionnaire is reproduced as appendix A.

Questionnaire survey approaches are rare in the literature of teaching styles, and it is instructive to consider the content and format of the questionnaire developed for this study in relation to other published sources. Only three other studies have been located, one British (Simon 1972) and two American (Adams 1970a; Walberg and Thomas 1971). This number is likely to increase, however. The Walberg and Thomas study is an investigation into 'open education', which, for the purpose of this discussion, is taken to be synonymous with 'progressive education' as defined in Plowden.

The Simon study is not directly comparable since it concentrated in greater depth on a narrower range of content. Nevertheless, although the questionnaires were developed concurrently, and in isolation, there is considerable overlap between them in certain areas such as classroom arrangement.

The Adams questionnaire was developed for a comparative survey of perceived teaching styles in the United Kingdom, Australia, New Zealand and the United States. The author isolated seven 'variable classes' from a review of traditional educational thinking which, he claimed, represent areas of generally widespread concern to teachers. They were: content orientation; cognitive emphasis; interaction mode; organisational differentiation; control source; control mode; and motivational mode. Each is described briefly below:

1 *Content orientation:* whether teaching emphasis is placed primarily on subject matter, on interpersonal relationships, or on discipline and control: in other words, whether the teaching is traditional, progressive or authoritarian

2 *Cognitive emphasis:* the kind of learning being promoted – the acquisition of skill, fact or understanding

3 *Interaction mode:* the communication pattern in the classroom; this encompasses three basic patterns – teacher dominated (lecture); teacher–pupil communication where teacher retains a measure of control; and free communication with no necessary teacher domination

4 *Organisational differentiation:* the way in which tasks are allocated and organised – whether all pupils are working on the same task collectively; differentiated groups working on the same task; or differentiated groups working on different tasks

5 *Control source:* whether classroom rules are determined by the teacher alone, by the teacher in collaboration with pupils or by pupils alone

6 *Control mode:* whether these rules are prescriptive, proscriptive or permissive

7 *Motivational mode:* whether intrinsic or extrinsic motivational procedures are manifest

These variable classes were operationalised by building items around the three categories in each. The twenty-one items were provided with five response categories relating to the degree of emphasis given in classroom teaching. The results of the survey are of little interest in the present context since the analysis simply compared teachers in the four countries on each variable class.

Walberg and Thomas (1971) were concerned that the concept 'open' had not been analysed into its component parts. They too carried out a review of traditional educational literature, and, in addition, of the analytic writings of Barth (1972), Bussis and Chittenden (1970) and Rathbone (1971). They finally isolated eight themes and built a fifty-item teacher questionnaire and rating scale around them. The eight themes and item representation are:

1 *Provisioning for learning:* range of materials supplied; freedom of pupil movement and talk; ability grouping; pupil choice of seating (twenty-five items)

2 *Humaneness:* materials developed by children; pupil abilities reflected in classroom environment; teacher care when dealing with conflicts (four items)

3 *Diagnosis of learning events:* regrouping of pupils on basis of test results; tests and assessment (four items)

4 *Instruction:* whether based on individual child; subject centred *v.* integration; lectures (five items)

5 *Evaluation of diagnostic information:* recording of cognitive and emotional development of pupils; teacher uses tests for comparative progress; evaluation as guide to instruction (five items)

6 *Seeking opportunities for professional growth:* teacher uses assistance of someone in supportive capacity; has helpful colleagues (two items)

7 *Self perception of teacher:* teacher tries to keep all her pupils in sight (one item)

8 *Assumptions about children and learning process:* warm emotional climate; clear guidelines given to class; children involved in what they are doing; emphasis on achievement (four items)

This questionnaire does not seem to be particularly satisfactory. The number of items representing each theme varies from twenty-five to one, with classroom management and organisation heavily overweighted. In addition to the problem of the validity of its content, there is the problem that the themes must differ greatly in reliability. Neither do the themes appear to be independent.

However, it is conceptual rather than constructional considerations which are of greater interest, and here the degree of overlap with this study in the content of the Adams and the Walberg and Thomas scale is very high, although they have been given different titles.

SAMPLING

Sampling considerations are paramount in an attempt to create valid typologies. Cluster techniques group people together who share common characteristics. If the sample is unrepresentative in terms of these characteristics the resultant typology will not be generalisable, and will consequently be of little utility.

A random sample of teachers taken on a national basis would have been the ideal sampling model, but the ideal is rarely possible given the limited resources of time, cost and staffing. Such was the case in this study. Instead it was decided to attempt a census of all third- and fourth-year primary teachers teaching in a given geographical area. For convenience this comprised the administrative counties of Lancashire and Cumbria.

Within this region can be found a wide range of school and environmental contexts, from schools whose intake areas cover the centres of industrial cities to those serving moorland villages, schools ranging in size of intake from four children to four forms, old schools and new schools, church schools and state schools – in all, an area rich in educational diversity.

The questionnaires were despatched to each headmaster in the 871 primary schools which serve the region. Included within the package were sufficient questionnaires for each relevant member of staff together with separate envelopes so that the class teacher could seal the completed questionnaire before returning it to the head teacher for despatch. This was designed to ensure complete confidentiality. A separate questionnaire was also included for the head teacher concerning school particulars and policy. Finally a stamped addressed envelope was provided for the return of all the questionnaires.

The packages were distributed to schools in late November and early December, despite the dictates of methodological folklore. Nevertheless 65 per cent of the schools had returned their questionnaires before the Christmas holidays, and by the end of January, after two follow-up letters, 88 per cent had responded, and a further 3 per cent had written explaining why they could not take part. This is an exceptionally high response rate for a postal survey and enables a high degree of confidence to be placed in the accuracy of the sample.

GENERAL TEACHING PATTERN

In order to assess whether age of class taught had any effect on the teaching style adopted, item response levels were computed separately for three levels – third year, third and fourth year mixed, and fourth year. The most striking feature of the result is the similarity of response pattern on most items, which suggests that in general teaching styles do not vary by age of pupils taught. The three groups were therefore combined to give the following general picture of primary school practice in upper primary schools.

Most teachers sit their pupils separately or in pairs rather than in larger groups, and most pupils remain in the same seats for most activities. Approximately one third of teachers use some form of internal streaming device by placing or grouping pupils on the basis of ability, whereas a similar proportion allow complete freedom in the choice of seating.

A high degree of permissiveness does not appear to be the norm in primary classrooms despite assertions to the contrary. Teacher control of physical movement and talk is generally high. Two thirds of teachers restrict these, a similar proportion expect their pupils to be quiet most of the time, and most require that pupils request permission to leave the room.

Responses to items concerning curriculum organisation also reflect a structured approach. In item 16 teachers were asked to indicate the emphasis placed on teacher talking to class as a whole, individual versus group work, and teacher-given versus pupil-chosen work. The results, in terms of the percentage of time devoted to each type of activity, are as follows:

Teacher talking to whole class	19%
Pupils working in groups on teacher tasks	21%
Pupils working in groups on tasks of own choice	10%
Pupils working individually on teacher tasks	37%
Pupils working individually on tasks of own choice	13%

These figures indicate that in general pupil work is teacher directed 77 per cent of the time and pupil directed 23 per cent of the time. Group work also seems to be much less favoured than individual work.

Other indications of structure include the fact that eight out of ten teachers require their pupils to know their multiplication tables off by heart, and one in three teachers give their pupils homework, although it should be noted that this is not so prevalent at third-year level, which possibly reflects the effect of the eleven-plus selection procedures at the later stage.

In addition a subject centred curriculum would seem to predominate. The teachers were asked to estimate the amount of time spent on all aspects of the curriculum in the last full week prior to completing the questionnaire. The average number of hours available for actual teaching each week has been found by Duthie (1970) to be twenty-five, and this was adopted as a standard. Three groupings were made of these data:

1 '*Academic*' *subjects taught separately:* included number work, English, reading, history, geography, French, science and scripture
2 '*Aesthetic*' *subjects:* included P.E. and games, music, art and craft, music and movement and drama
3 '*Integrated*' *subjects:* included environmental studies, social studies, project and topic work, free choice periods and other integrated work

Of the twenty-five hours, fifteen and a quarter were devoted to academic subjects, five to aesthetic subjects, and four and three quarters to all forms of integrated subjects.

Despite the subject centred approach there does seem to be a move towards emphasising fluency and originality in written work, even if this is achieved at the expense of grammatical accuracy. Nevertheless spelling and grammatical errors are usually corrected even if few teachers assign an actual grade to pupils' work. Assessment of work in the shape of tests of arithmetic and spelling take place each week, and over half the teachers set end-of-term tests.

Discipline does not appear to be a problem at the primary level. Less than one in ten teachers claim to have many pupils who create discipline problems, and over 95 per cent find that verbal reproof is normally sufficient to deal with such problems. Nevertheless, for persistent disruptive behaviour a number of other measures are used, the most common being withdrawal of privileges, extra work and smacking. It was somewhat surprising to find that over half the teachers admitted to smacking when it appears to be frowned on at the official level.

This general picture, although of interest, does not provide information about the range of teaching approaches adopted by teachers. In order to isolate the variety of these styles a cluster analysis was undertaken. This is a useful technique since it allows people to be grouped together who have similar characteristics, in this instance teachers who had a similar profile of responses to all the questionnaire items. These groupings are often denoted 'types', which McQuitty (1967) defines as categories of persons such that every person in the category is more like every other person in the category than he is like any other person in any other category. The cluster analysis is based on the 468 fourth year teachers, and is described further by Bennett (1975) and Bennett and Jordan (1975).

Twelve teacher types or styles were extracted from the cluster analysis, and can be described as follows:

Type 1

These teachers favour integration of subject matter, and, unlike most other groups, allow pupil choice of work, whether undertaken individually or in groups. Most allow pupils choice of seating. Less than half curb movement and talk. Assessment in all its forms – tests, grading, and homework – appears to be discouraged. Intrinsic motivation is favoured.

Type 2

These teachers also prefer integration of subject matter. Teacher control appears to be low, but the teachers offer less pupil choice of work. However, most allow pupils choice of seating, and only one third curb movement and talk. Few test or grade work.

Type 3

The main teaching mode of this group is class teaching and group work. Integration of subject matter is preferred, and is associated with taking their pupils out of school. These teachers appear to be strict, most curbing movement and talk, and offenders are smacked. The amount of testing is average, but the amount of grading and homework below average.

Type 4

These teachers prefer separate subject teaching but a high proportion allow pupil choice of work both in group and individual work. None seat their pupils by ability. They test and grade more than average.

Type 5

A mixture of separate subject and integrated subject teaching is characteristic of this group. The main teaching mode is pupils working in groups of their own choice on tasks set by the teacher. Teacher talk is lower than average. Control is high with regard to movement but not to talk. Most give tests every week and many give homework regularly. Stars are rarely used, and pupils are taken out of school regularly.

Type 6

These teachers prefer to teach subjects separately with emphasis on groups working on teacher-specified tasks. The amount of individual work is small. These teachers appear to be fairly low on control, and in the use of extrinsic motivation.

Type 7

This group are separate subject orientated, with a high level of class teaching together with individual work. Teacher control appears to be tight, few teachers allow movement or choice of seating, and offenders are smacked. Assessment, however, is low.

Type 8

This group of teachers has very similar characteristics to those of type 3, the difference being that these prefer to organise the work on an individual rather than a group basis. Freedom of movement is restricted, and most expect pupils to be quiet.

Type 9

These teachers favour separate subject teaching, the predominant teaching mode being individuals working on tasks set by the teacher. Teacher control appears to be high; most curb movement and talk, and seat by ability. Pupil choice is minimal. regular spelling tests are given, but few mark or grade work, or use stars.

Type 10

All these teachers favour separate subject teaching. The teaching mode favoured is teacher talk to whole class, and pupils working in groups determined by the teacher, on tasks set by the teacher. Most curb movement and talk, and over two thirds smack for disruptive behaviour. There is regular testing and most give stars for good work.

Type 11

All members of this group stress separate subject teaching by way of class teaching and individual work. Pupil choice of work is minimal, although most teachers allow choice in seating. Movement and talk are curbed, and offenders smacked.

Type 12

This is an extreme group in a number of respects. None favour an integrated approach. Subjects are taught separately by class teaching and individual work. None allow pupils choice of seating, and every teacher curbs movement and talk. These teachers are above average on all assessment procedures, and extrinsic motivation predominates.

The types have been subjectively ordered, for descriptive purposes, in order of distance from the most 'informal' cluster (type 1). This suggests that they can be represented by points on a continuum of 'informal–formal', but this would be an over-simplification. The extreme types could be adequately described in these terms, but the remaining types all contain both informal and formal elements.

VALIDATION

This analysis provides an indication that the ubiquitous use of dichotomous descriptions of teaching styles fails to take into account the multiplicity of elements involved. When construed unidimensionally on the progressive–traditional range, only a minority of styles are adequately described. The majority of teachers appear to adopt a mixed or intermediate style for which the progressive–traditional dimension provides inadequate description.

However, the claim that the above typology provides a more adequate description of classroom reality is of little value unless it can be established that the classification is valid. Evidence of validity has therefore been sought from three sources: ratings by research staff; ratings by local authority advisers; and descriptions of the school day by the pupils.

Thirty-seven teachers whose responses most closely matched the central profiles of seven of the twelve clusters (see chapter 5) agreed to participate in the second stage of the project, and it is from these teachers that evidence concerning validity has been derived. Research staff spent two days in each of the classrooms during the course of data collection, and on their return were asked to write a description of each classroom based on the items in the questionnaire and cluster analysis. Although they were unaware of the cluster membership of the teachers, their reports related closely to the cluster descriptions.

The second source of evidence was gained from the L.E.A. advisers. All the primary school advisers from all of the participating authorities attended a meeting at which the questionnaire, the analysis, and the cluster descriptions were discussed. Although the thirty-seven teachers were already known to them, the advisers agreed to visit each teacher in their authority again and report their observations in terms of the questionnaire items and cluster descriptions. Again, the cluster membership of each teacher was unknown to them. An analysis of these reports indicated an 80 per cent agreement between their ratings and the cluster description.

Of interest was the fact that the research staff and the advisers isolated the same two instances where the way in which the teacher said he taught did not correspond too closely with how he was actually teaching. Fortunately these were isolated cases, and other indications are that response bias did not operate widely. The fact that the analysis delineated so few progressive teachers when there appears to be pressure to teach in this manner, and that so many teachers admitted to smacking when this is discouraged both by the L.E.A.s and the N.U.T., are indications of this.

The third, and perhaps most interesting, source of evidence is that gained from content analyses of an essay written by all the pupils in the thirty-seven classes entitled 'What I did at school yesterday'. In this the pupils were asked to record as accurately as possible all that had happened at school the previous day. Nine classrooms have been analysed. Initially two assistants were given the essays from the same class and were asked to provide independent descriptions of the classroom. The two descriptions were virtually identical, indicating a very high interjudge agreement. Brief descriptions of two classrooms are reported to indicate the type of data gained from this approach.

Class A (class teacher: Mrs B)

Mrs B allows her children freedom of choice and of movement before school officially begins and before she enters the room, and this freedom is mirrored elsewhere in the school day. Most of the children begin the day with verbal reasoning, though a few work in books titled *Objective English* and *Word Perfect*. When they have completed verbal reasoning, the first choice point in the day occurs. As Andrew E. explains it, 'we did verble resoning. After working a bit we could finish our paintings. But I did clay modeling with Paul C. And he made an awful mess . . .' While some children were building models and painting, others were working on projects such as fossils and water, while still others worked on *Objective English* or *Word Perfect*. The choice which children have here seems a real choice, without teacher 'management'; most of the children have finished their work before assembly and have time for a second activity.

After assembly and playtime, children who have not already done so are expected to finish off the verbal reasoning. Then they may select an activity, again with no apparent management from Mrs B. The thirty-nine pupils split into ten activities including *Word Perfect*, *Objective English*, projects, modelling (apparently from oddments), a play (involving three girls), sewing soft toys, making collages for an exhibition, drawing, clay work, and maths. The children take an especially active interest in the work during this period; both evaluative and descriptive comments were prevalent:

Then after maths I started to do a drawing about a war. The drawing had a main aircraft which had rockets on it. (Andrew G.)

After playtime I started on the ship with David H. I made some brilliant steps for it. The ship was called the Graf Spee. (Christopher H.)

Then Stephen and I did some clay modelling. I did a waterfall, but I didn't turn out right so I demolished it. (Jonathan S.)

Then I did a play with Mary and Debbie, Debbie got Mandy and went away so Mary and I did it by ourself. We didn't do it all so we are going to finish it off tomorrow. (Louise B.)

Louise's comment indicates a firm expectation that tomorrow will once again include periods for pupil choice.

The choice period ends and the pupils move to one of the three reading groups taken by Mr A., Mr K. and Mrs B. The children know which group to join, but it is not clear on what basis the groups are formed. This continues until lunch.

After lunch a short time is spent going over homework. A quiz follows which had been requested by Stephen L. during the morning. This indicates that the pupils as well as the teacher are able to influence curriculum activity. The whole class are involved and it develops into a competition of boys versus girls.

During the last period most of the children are involved in a rehearsal for a Christmas play. The pupils who are not in the play can apparently choose what they would like to do in the classroom.

The degree of pupil choice in this classroom appears particularly high. All children had at least one choice period, during the morning between playtime and reading. Most of the children had a second choice period just before morning assembly, and a few had a third choice time at the end of the day when the others were practising the Christmas play. Also all of the children had the opportunity for choice before school began, when at least seven different activities were available without teacher supervision.

Class A was delineated as type 1 by the cluster analysis, but this class was deliberately chosen for detailed report here for another reason: it highlights the effect of external factors or pressures on the teaching decisions taken. It may seem incongruous to some that a progressive teacher begins the day with verbal reasoning practice, and sets homework. However, this is explained by the fact that the school is in an area which has retained the eleven-plus selection procedure. Separate analyses have been carried out relating factors such as the presence of selective examinations, size of school, church affiliation and type of intake area, to teaching style adopted, and are described more fully in chapter 4.

Class B (class teacher: Mr M)

Before school a few of the boys play football in the playground, while one child goes into the building to open windows. After assembly their teacher Mr M. 'gave us some of our marks from the test we had just took' (Pauline F.) until Mrs P. arrived to teach the class English.

After playtime, the class has French with Mrs H. 'who is the school only french teacher' (Ian C.). According to Andrew F. they 'learnt how to wright the numbers in French'.

After French Mr M. returned to take part of the class swimming while 'the rest stay behind with Mrs P. doing Topic work' (Beverley H.). The topics were apparently determined by the individual students; Suzanne M.'s topic book 'is on Ballet'. She later comments: 'when playtime finished I left school because I went to my Ballet Exam at 3.00. Most of my friends hoped that I would do well.'

After dinnertime Mr M. 'gave out the names of the people who came in the Top Ten (Suzanne M.). Several of the children reported positioning, and the exam results took up two periods in the day. Andrew F. reports: 'then at 2.10 we went down to the hall and had P.E. We played a game called dogge ball . . . Red's won every game, and I am in the Reds.' After P.E. and playtime, the class wrote the composition 'Invisible for a day' (this was for the project).

When we came in Mr. M. told us to get just our pencils out and I thought oh here we go another test. It was not a test it was a composition we had to write just like this one. (Nichola W.)

We went in and wrote a composition about an Invisible day I made my
story as funny as I could snipping strings of balloons making bottle of
washing up liquid dance and frightening people I had fun writing it
and pretending to be Sylvia (Julie T.)

In contrast to class A no choice period is offered to pupils in
this class. Choice within a session is only offered once, i.e. for
topic work, but this almost seemed to be a 'filler' while the
remainder of the class went swimming. Except for this period
the class was taught as a whole throughout the day. There is an
obvious emphasis on testing, extrinsic motivation and competition. Class B was delineated type 12 by the cluster analysis.

The content and sequence of the school day in classes A and B
is presented in summary form in figure 3.1.

These brief outlines fail to do justice to the richness of the
original descriptions. Nevertheless, sufficient has been reported
to demonstrate the type of information gained, and to indicate
the usefulness of the technique as a complement to other approaches. For example, Hargreaves (1972) has argued that interaction analysis fails to explore the assumptions and perspectives
of teachers and pupils.

We discover little of the overall teacher–pupil relationship as it is
experienced by the teacher or by individual pupils. Yet it is this
relationship which may not only influence the meaning assigned to
particular verbal statements or acts, but also exercise a pervasive influence which is not immediately obvious or directly open to measurement by traditional methods.

Content analysis of relevant pupil output could provide this
sort of information. According to Kerlinger (1973), content
analysis is a method of observation. 'Instead of observing people's
behaviour directly, or asking them to respond to scales, or in-
terviewing them, the investigator takes the communications that
people have produced, and asks questions of the communicator.'
In this instance classroom action has been observed through the
eyes of the pupils, a method which would appear to have certain
advantages. It can, for example, be considered a low inference
procedure: an activity occurs, the children involved report it,
the investigator tallies it and incorporates it in the description.

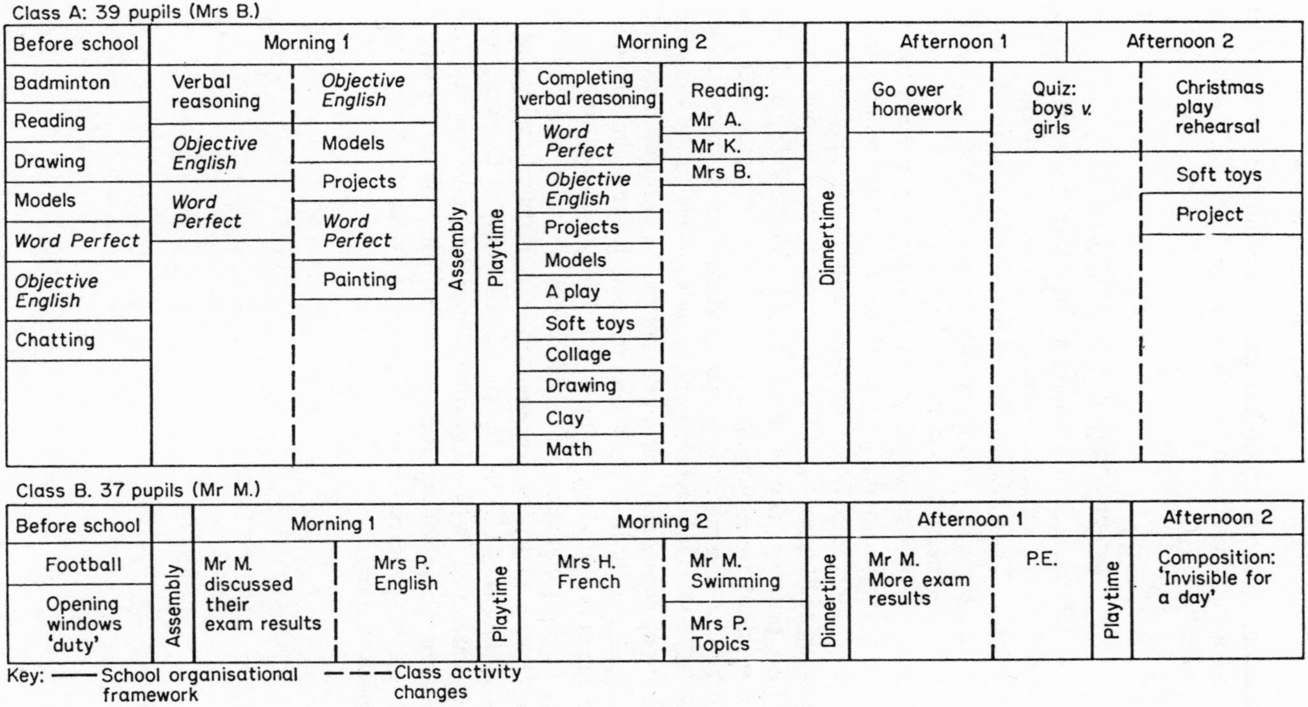

Class A: 39 pupils (Mrs B.)

Before school	Morning 1		Morning 2		Afternoon 1		Afternoon 2
Badminton	Verbal reasoning	Objective English	Completing verbal reasoning	Reading: Mr A.	Go over homework	Quiz: boys v. girls	Christmas play rehearsal
Reading	Objective English	Models	Word Perfect	Mr K.			Soft toys
Drawing	Projects		Objective English	Mrs B.			Project
Models	Word Perfect		Projects				
Word Perfect		Painting	Models				
Objective English			A play				
Chatting			Soft toys				
			Collage				
			Drawing				
			Clay				
			Math				

(Assembly and Playtime between Morning 1 and Morning 2; Dinnertime between Morning 2 and Afternoon 1)

Class B. 37 pupils (Mr M.)

Before school	Morning 1		Morning 2		Afternoon 1		Afternoon 2
Football	Mr M. discussed their exam results	Mrs P. English	Mrs H. French	Mr M. Swimming	Mr M. More exam results	P.E.	Composition: 'Invisible for a day'
Opening windows 'duty'				Mrs P. Topics			

(Assembly before Morning 1; Playtime after Morning 1; Dinnertime between Morning 2 and Afternoon 1; Playtime in Afternoon 1)

Key: —— School organisational framework   ––– Class activity changes

Figure 3.1 *Content and sequence of the school day for class A and class B*

Since often some thirty children are describing the same event the resulting description would seem to have high reliability and validity.

POSTSCRIPT TO PLOWDEN

The cluster analysis of teaching styles makes possible a comparison between current practice, and current conceptions of that practice. The Plowden Report described a pattern of teaching which, it maintained, represented a general and quickening trend. This pattern was set out in chapter 1.

Later writers have attempted to quantify this 'general trend'. Blackie (1967) maintained that a third of primary schools were working along these lines, and Silberman (1970), drawing upon the work of Rogers (1970) felt safe in saying that 25 per cent of English primary schools fitted the Plowden model, and that another third were moving towards it. Simon's study did not substantiate this trend however, and neither do the findings reported here. Only type 1 corresponds closely to the Plowden definition, containing just 9 per cent of the population studied. A separate analysis of third year teachers isolated similar types, and the corresponding group at this level contained only 8 per cent of the population. It could of course be argued that the sample studied is not representative of primary teachers as a whole. This may be true, but the H.M.I. study of teaching practices, contained in the Plowden Report, found little regional variation. These findings together with those provided by Simon indicate that progressive teaching is less prevalent than has hitherto been supposed.

4

Teacher aims and opinions

It has been argued that the attitudes teachers hold are intimately related to their effectiveness in the classroom situation. For example if the class teacher does not share the head teacher's beliefs about methods of teaching and organisation then these methods may not receive a fair trial (Tupper 1965). On the same theme Barker Lunn labelled as 'misfits' those teachers who taught in a manner different from their underlying educational philosophy. Teacher attitudes may thus be seen to be an important factor in the teaching situation although there is as yet little evidence to substantiate this. Most previous research has concentrated on tracing the relationships between attitudes and age, sex, and age level taught. From such studies it would seem that younger teachers and primary teachers have more favourable attitudes towards informal teaching approaches, and there is a little evidence to suggest that men favour informality more than women (Ryans 1960; Peterson 1964; Tupper 1965; Morrison and McIntyre 1967; Barker Lunn 1970). Nevertheless, there is very little research concerning the extent to which attitudes relate to overt teaching behaviour.

In order to investigate this link between attitudes and behaviour three questionnaires were developed to assess teaching aims, opinions about educational issues, and opinions about teaching methods (appendix A). The items were derived from other research studies and from interviews with teachers.

The following general picture of aims and opinions is based on the responses of those 468 teachers on which the typology of teaching styles was created.

TEACHING AIMS

The rubric for the teaching aims section was 'The following are probably all worthwhile aims but their relative importance may be influenced by the situation in which the teacher works. Please rate each aim on the five point scale to indicate its importance in relation to your class.' The five point scale ranged from 'Not important' to 'Essential'. The teachers placed these aims in the order of importance shown in table 4.1.

A separate analysis of teaching head teachers gave an almost identical ranking.

The data show teaching aims divided into three basic groups – one essential aim, six very important aims and two important or fairly important aims. There is a high degree of consensus that the acquisition of basic skills in reading and number is essential, 81 per cent of teachers regarding this as so. However, this concern for basic skills is in marked contrast to the other two aims involving academic work which rank eighth and ninth. One in five teachers regarded the promotion of a high level of academic attainment as not important and a further 25 per cent thought it to be only fairly important. Most of the aims regarded as very important come in the area of social and moral development, and it is thus of interest to compare these ratings with those gained by Taylor and Holley (1975) in a more extensive study of aims in primary education. The studies are somewhat different in that a more extensive list of aims was presented to teachers by Taylor and Holley, who asked teachers to assess their own contribution to the achievement of the aims. The stance that teachers were required to take was to assess their differential contribution to the achievement of aims rather than to assess the differential importance of the aims themselves. Nevertheless the findings do show points of overlap. The aims consistently in the top ten were related to social and moral development rather than to intellectual development. These aims related to the child being happy at school, enjoying school work, being careful with and respectful of other people's property, and acquiring a set of moral values. However, further down this list creeps in the necessity that a child should read fluently, accurately and with understanding.

The general picture painted by the findings of both these

Teaching Aims	Mean Score	Not important	Fairly important	Important	Very important	Essential
1 The acquisition of basic skills in reading and number work	4·8	—	—	3	16	81
2 The acceptance of normal standards of behaviour	4·2	—	2	19	33	46
3 Helping pupils to cooperate with each other	4·0	—	3	22	40	34
4 An understanding of the world in which pupils live	3·9	1	4	31	31	32
5 The enjoyment of school	3·9	—	7	25	36	31
6 The encouragement of self-expression	3·8	—	3	22	40	23
7 The development of pupils creative abilities	3·7	—	6	34	41	18
8 Preparation for academic work in secondary school	3·0	7	24	44	15	10
9 The promotion of a high level of academic attainment	2·6	18	24	41	13	4

Table 4.1 *Teaching aims in order of perceived importance*

Note Percentages in this table and other tables may total more than 100 as a result of rounding up.

studies is one in which basic skills are stressed within an environment which allows for self-expression and cooperation. Teachers
do not see junior schools as agents of preparation for secondary
education and seemingly emphasise social and moral, rather than
intellectual, development.

OPINIONS ABOUT EDUCATION ISSUES

Many of the opinions on this section of the questionnaire were
those that had been voiced by teachers in interviews or had been
published by protagonists of both progressive and traditional
teaching. The teachers were, in this instance, asked to indicate the
strength of their agreement or disagreement with the opinions
expressed in the statements. Originally the scale ranged from
'strongly agree' to 'strongly disagree' but an unfortunate printing
error necessitated a shift to a three point scale – agree, no opinion,
disagree. The opinions are listed below in order of consensus of
agreement (table 4.2). For example 95 per cent of teachers agreed
that 'Teachers need to know the home background and personal
circumstances of their pupils' whilst at the other end of the scale
71 per cent disagreed that 'Creativity is an educational fad which
could soon die out.'

These items do not constitute a scale in the normally accepted
sense of that term: they are really a collection of statements some
of which could be considered to be contentious. However, broad
agreement is indicated on five of these. Knowledge is required
about pupils' background; teachers should be liked by the class;
creativity is not a fad; pupils feel secure in a structured teaching
environment; and firm teacher discipline leads to good self-
discipline on the part of the pupil. However, the rest of the
answers point to major splits of opinion, most interestingly perhaps on the question of streaming. Streamed primary schools are
in the minority in Britain today – only 13 per cent of the schools
approached in the survey were streamed – yet 31 per cent of
teachers feel that streaming by ability is desirable. This would
seem to support Barker Lunn's idea of teacher 'misfits', since
many more teachers have pro-streaming attitudes than there are
streamed schools.

The remaining four statements refer to the internal organisa-

Opinions about educational issues	Disagree	No opinion	Agree
1 Teachers need to know the home background and personal circumstances of their pupils	3	2	95
2 The teacher should be well liked by the class	6	16	78
3 Most pupils in upper junior school feel more secure if told what to do and how to do it	13	3	83
4 Firm discipline by the teacher leads to good self-discipline on the part of the pupils	18	9	73
5 Streaming by ability is undesirable in a junior school	31	9	60
6 Too little emphasis is placed on keeping order in the classroom nowadays	34	13	53
7 Pupils work better when motivated by marks or stars	35	15	50
8 Most pupils in upper junior school have sufficient maturity to choose a topic to study and carry it through	53	11	37
9 Children working in groups waste a lot time arguing and 'messing about'	53	11	37
10 Creativity is an educational fad which could soon die out	71	17	12

Table 4.2 *Order of agreement of opinions about educational issues*

tion of teaching in the classroom. From the responses it is fairly clear that it is here at the 'chalk face' that attitudes are most polarised. The question of whether pupils have sufficient maturity to choose a topic and carry it through lies at the heart of discovery learning approaches. If pupils do not have this maturity then such teaching approaches are vitiated, and the rejection of this statement by almost half the teachers would suggest a fairly high degree of antipathy to such methods.

Approximately half of the teachers accept the view that too little emphasis is placed on keeping order in the classroom, which perhaps reflects a concern that the teacher's traditional authority is being threatened by the move towards more informal practices. The same percentage are in favour of extrinsic motivational techniques such as stars. It will be noted that extrinsic versus intrinsic motivation is one of the elements which supposedly differentiates formal and informal methods. In this sample the more formal practices are obviously preferred. Finally the statement relating to group work is one often heard when teachers discuss methods, but in this instance half disagree with the notion that group work leads to less work-related activity.

The polarity of opinions on statements pertaining to teaching styles can be further explicated by a consideration of the final area investigated, opinions about teaching methods.

OPINIONS ABOUT TEACHING METHODS

The format of this section (table 4.3) diverged from that of the two sections considered above because teachers were requested to agree or disagree with the same statement when applied to (a) formal teaching methods and (b) informal teaching methods.

Statement 1 is the only one that makes reference to the teacher and the demands made upon him by the method adopted. Quite clearly teachers perceive informal teaching as making much greater demands on the teacher. 91 per cent agree with the statement in relation to informal teaching methods whereas only 35 per cent state agreement in relation to formal methods.

Statement 2 relates to classroom structure, and reflected in the statement is the fear that informal methods could result in a rather inchoate classroom organisation which leaves pupils unsure of what to do. In fact 62 per cent of teachers felt that this did occur in informal teaching. On the other hand 81 per cent disagreed with the statement that this was the case with formal methods.

Statement 3 reflects another commonly held belief, that informal teaching could lead to excessive pupil freedom, and perhaps result in problems of discipline. This belief is supported by the teacher responses, 77 per cent agreeing that informal methods

Opinions about teaching methods	Formal methods					Informal methods				
	Strongly disagree	Disagree	No opinion	Agree	Strongly agree	Strongly disagree	Disagree	No opinion	Agree	Strongly agree
1 Make heavy demands on teacher	9	45	11	30	5	1	4	3	43	48
2 Leave many pupils unsure of what to do	16	65	8	10	2	1	26	10	49	13
3 Could create discipline problems	14	51	10	24	1	3	15	6	66	11
4 Encourage time wasting or day dreaming	15	59	13	11	1	2	32	13	44	9
5 Teach pupils to think for themselves	10	34	20	33	3	0	7	14	62	16
6 Teach basic skills and concepts effectively	1	10	6	60	23	7	37	16	37	2
7 Encourage responsibility and self-discipline	7	33	18	38	3	1	14	15	56	14
8 Allow each child to develop his full potential	10	35	16	36	3	2	23	19	46	10
9 Provide right balance between teaching and individual work	6	28	19	39	7	1	24	24	45	6
10 Fail to bring the best out of bright pupils	12	50	8	25	4	8	53	13	21	5

Table 4.3 *Opinions about teaching methods* (The statements in this table are ordered in terms of greatest discrepancy of rating between formal and informal methods.)

could engender discipline problems, and 65 per cent feeling that this is not likely to occur under formal teaching.

The effects of lack of structure on pupils also underlies statement 4, since another commonly held view is that informal teaching, if poorly organised, leads to time wasting. The majority of teachers would seem to share this feeling. 53 per cent agreed that this is likely under informal teaching whereas 74 per cent felt that it would not occur under formal methods.

Teaching pupils to think for themselves is one of the major aims of informal schooling, the ultimate objective being independent learning on the part of the pupil. This view was given strong support, 78 per cent agreeing that informal methods do enable pupils to think for themselves. Teachers were somewhat equivocal about this statement in relation to formal methods, 36 per cent claiming that formal methods also perform this function and 44 per cent disagreeing.

Statement 6 relates to an area where formal teachers feel their methods are more effective. Again this was strongly supported, 83 per cent agreeing that formal methods allow basic skills and concepts to be taught effectively, whereas opinion on this question was split almost equally with regard to informal methods, 44 per cent disagreeing with the statement and 39 per cent agreeing.

Statement 7 relates to another area where it is often held that better development occurs under informal teaching, and the pattern of responses closely parallels that of statement 5. 70 per cent of teachers feel that informal methods encourage responsibility and self-discipline, whilst opinions are almost equally divided about this in relation to formal methods.

On statements 8, 9 and 10 there is little discrepancy between methods although slightly more teachers feel that informal methods allow the pupil to develop his full potential. From responses to statements 9 and 10 it would appear that both formal and informal methods are equally effective or ineffective in providing the right balance between teaching and individual work, and bringing out the best in bright pupils.

The opinion of the majority of teachers about the pros and cons of formal and informal methods is summarised in the following table.

Formal methods	Informal methods
Do not make heavy demands on teachers	Make heavy demands on teachers
Do not leave pupils unsure of what to do	Leave pupils unsure of what to do
Teach basic skills and concepts effectively	Teach pupils to think for themselves
Unlikely to create discipline problems	Could create discipline problems
Unlikely to encourage time wasting or day dreaming	Likely to encourage time wasting and day dreaming
	Encourage responsibility and self-discipline
	Allow child to develop his full potential

Further analyses were carried out to assess the effect of age and sex on opinions about teaching methods. These indicated that women teachers have slightly less favourable attitudes to informal methods, and that teachers over the age of forty are also likely to favour more formal approaches, bearing out the results of earlier research.

AIMS AND OPINIONS COMPARED WITH TEACHING STYLES

Few studies have attempted to relate the aims and opinions of teachers to the way they actually teach. A recent attempt was that of Ashton and others (1975), but the study was limited to a questionnaire survey, an indication of teaching method being given by a single item whereby teachers had to pick one of five alternatives. Nevertheless this gave a crude indication and produced some interesting findings. Clear relationships were found between teaching approach, teachers' opinions about the broad purposes of education, and the aspects of children's development which they considered to be least and most important in education. The authors summarised their findings as follows:

Those teachers who considered that the broad purpose of primary education is to equip children with skills and attitudes, which will enable them to fit effectively and competently into society, tended to stress as most important children's intellectual, moral, physical and spiritual development; they also tended to choose to work in a more traditional, teacher directed manner with the accent on the acquisition of basic skills and knowledge to specified levels of achievement. Those teachers who considered that the broad purpose of primary education is to develop children's independence and individuality, enabling them to discover their own talents and interests and to arrive at their own enjoyment and attitudes towards society, were markedly inclined to stress as most important the aesthetic and emotional/personal aspects of development; they tended to choose to work in a more progressive, child centred manner with the accent on inquiry and the acquisition of basic skills as the children require them at their own pace.

It was thus strongly suggested that teachers' opinions about modes of teaching are firmly rooted in their fundamental views about the aims of education.

Age differences were also apparent in that the more traditionally inclined tended to be older, more experienced and married, whereas the more progressively oriented tended to be younger, less experienced and single. Few sex differences were found.

To assess the relationship between opinion and practice, the responses of the teachers in each of the twelve teaching styles were computed for each item of the sections on aims, on opinions about education issues and on opinions about teaching methods. These response patterns are presented in appendix B. Following this the responses of the teachers in the seven teaching styles used in the second stage of the study were computed and collapsed into the three categories of informal, mixed and formal (table 4.4).

The aims can be broadly categorised as academic (A, B, C, D and I) and social (E, F, G and H). Of the five academic aims there is broad agreement on two: 'an understanding of the world in which pupils live', where approximately one-third state that this is essential and a slightly higher proportion feel it to be very important, and 'the acquisition of basic skills in reading and number work', although somewhat more emphasis is placed on this aim by formal and mixed teachers.

Aims A and I are of interest since they represent the only two items where an appreciable proportion expressed the view that they were not important. No less than half of the informal teachers rated 'preparation for academic work in secondary schools' as unimportant or fairly important, and only 11 per cent

		Informal					Mixed					Formal			
		1	2	3	4	5	1	2	3	4	5	1	2	3	4	5
A	Preparation for academic work in secondary school	12	39	38	8	3	8	21	47	20	7	2	13	43	23	21
B	An understanding of the world in which pupils live	0	5	26	42	28	1	2	27	33	30	2	7	28	35	29
C	The acquisition of basic skills in reading and number work	0	0	10	18	73	1	0	1	14	84	0	0	0	14	86
D	The development of pupil's creative abilities	0	2	20	47	23	1	3	42	38	16	2	10	41	37	11
E	The encouragement of self-expression	0	2	27	38	33	0	2	33	46	19	2	11	41	33	14
F	Helping pupils to cooperate with one another	3	2	20	37	38	0	3	18	45	34	0	4	28	45	24
G	The acceptance of normal standards of behaviour	3	3	27	30	37	0	1	11	45	43	0	2	22	22	55
H	The enjoyment of school	2	6	20	31	43	0	8	28	34	29	3	14	28	36	20
I	The promotion of a high level of academic attainment	18	28	45	8	2	19	25	43	8	4	13	23	38	21	7

Table 4.4 *The responses of informal, mixed and formal teachers to statements about aims*

Key 1 Not important 2 Fairly important 3 Important 4 Very important 5 Essential

thought it to be very important or essential. This is almost the reverse of the view expressed by formal teachers, 44 per cent of whom rated it as very important or essential. The responses of the mixed teachers were somewhere between these extremes. This same pattern is also apparent for 'the promotion of a high level of academic attainment', although to a less marked extent.

The response pattern for the final academic aim, 'the development of a pupil's creative abilities', was similar for formal and mixed teachers, who placed less emphasis on this than informal teachers.

Of the four aims in the social area two elicited broad agreement with only slight differences in emphasis. Approximately 70 per cent of teachers in each style rated 'helping pupils to cooperate with each other' as very important or essential, with a slightly greater emphasis on the part of informal teachers. This pattern is also true of 'the enjoyment of school', the strength of response falling progressively from informal, through mixed, to formal teachers. 74 per cent of informal teachers feel this aim to be very important or essential, compared with 63 per cent of mixed teachers and 56 per cent of formal teachers.

It is clear that informal and mixed teachers are more concerned to encourage self-expression, 71 per cent and 65 per cent respectively rating this as very important or essential compared with 47 per cent of formal teachers. But if the pattern of responses to 'the acceptance of normal standards of behaviour' is noted it is clear that as far as mixed teachers are concerned this cannot be equated with a free-for-all situation. 87 per cent stress that such standards are very important or essential compared with 67 per cent of informal teachers.

In summary, there are basic agreements among fourth-year junior teachers that their pupils should acquire basic skills in reading and number work, that pupils should acquire an understanding of the world in which they live, that they as teachers should help pupils to cooperate with each other, and that pupils should enjoy school.

Formal teachers stress far more their role in preparing children for academic work in secondary school and in the promotion of a high level of attainment generally. In both these areas mixed teachers come midway between formal and informal teachers.

Formal and mixed teachers are less inclined to rate the development of creative abilities highly and are more concerned with inculcating the acceptance of normal standards of behaviour in their pupils. However informal and mixed teachers hold in common the belief that self-expression should be encouraged.

The results are thus as might be expected in view of the study by Ashton and others.

OPINIONS ABOUT EDUCATIONAL ISSUES

Both the Plowden Report and the Ashton study noted that teachers were more adept at passing opinions than at stating clear aims. It might therefore be posited that even greater divergence would appear on opinions about educational issues than was apparent on aims. Table 4.5 provides the responses to the ten statements arranged by teaching style, and appendix B contains the responses for all teachers.

A study of table 4.5 will show that there are three basic groupings

		Informal			Formal			Mixed		
		D	N	A	D	N	A	D	N	A
A	Most pupils in upper junior school have sufficient maturity to choose a topic to study and carry it through	41	5	56	52	3	45	54	1	45
B	Most pupils in upper junior school feel more secure if told what to do and how to do it	31	2	68	9	2	90	10	4	87
C	Creativity is an educational fad which could soon die out	88	10	3	64	21	16	68	19	13
D	Firm discipline by the teacher leads to good self-discipline on the part of the pupils	35	13	53	9	7	85	14	7	80
E	Streaming by ability is undesirable in junior school	20	8	74	40	13	48	36	10	54
F	The teacher should be well liked by the class	6	14	81	9	25	67	5	15	80
G	Children working in groups waste a lot of time arguing and 'messing about'	76	8	17	32	12	57	48	16	36
H	Pupils work better when motivated by marks or stars	62	17	22	13	9	80	32	23	45
I	Too little emphasis is placed on keeping order in the classroom nowadays	58	15	28	15	14	70	28	13	59
J	Teachers need to know the home background and personal circumstances of their pupils	3	0	97	3	7	91	5	1	94

Table 4.5 *Opinions about educational issues by teaching style* (D = Disagree, N = No opinion, A = Agree)

of opinions: those where there is broad agreement across teaching styles; those where there is a discrepancy of opinion across teaching styles; and those where there is divergence of opinion within teaching styles.

The statement on which the clearest agreement is shown is 'Teachers need to know the home background and personal circumstances of their pupils', over 90 per cent of teachers in each style agreeing with the statement. Most teachers also agree that they should be well liked by their class although this is less marked among formal teachers. This is also true of the statement that 'Creativity is an educational fad which could soon die out.' 88 per cent of informal teachers disagree with this statement whereas approximately two-thirds of formal and mixed teachers do so. Mixed and formal teachers also align together on the issue that 'Most pupils feel more secure if told what to do and how to do it.' Nine out of ten formal and mixed teachers agree compared with seven out of ten informal teachers.

The four statements which show the greatest disagreement according to teaching approach relate to two areas, discipline and modes of pupil work. On statement D, 'Firm discipline by the teacher leads to good self-discipline on the part of the pupils', over 80 per cent of formal and mixed teachers agreed compared with just over 50 per cent of informal teachers. There is some indication of disagreement within the informal teachers' group here since 35 per cent disagreed with the statement. Item I refers to discipline, stating that 'Too little emphasis is placed on order nowadays', and here there are marked disagreements. 70 per cent of formal, 59 per cent of mixed and only 28 per cent of informal teachers agreed with this, and 58 per cent of informal teachers disagreed.

On modes of pupil work item G, 'Children working in groups waste a lot of time', demonstrates a similar cleavage. 76 per cent of informal, 48 per cent of mixed and only 32 per cent of formal teachers disagree with the statement. On the other hand 57 per cent of formal teachers felt that group work did indeed waste a lot of time. Statement H reflects the extrinsic and intrinsic motivation argument, stating that 'Pupils work better when motivated by marks or stars.' As might be expected, 80 per cent of formal teachers agree, compared with 45 per cent of mixed and 22 per cent of informal teachers. 62 per cent of informal teachers disagreed.

On two statements there seems to be marked disagreement within teaching styles. These relate to streaming and pupil maturity. The informal teachers are quite clearly opposed to streaming in the ratio 4:1 but there is a large measure of disagreement among mixed and formal teachers. 54 per cent of mixed teachers were against and 36 per cent for, and among formal teachers the situation was more equivocal, 48 per cent being against and 40 per cent for.

The extent of disagreement among teachers with similar teaching styles was even more evident in relation to statement A, 'Most pupils have sufficient maturity to choose a topic to study and carry it through.' 56 per cent of informal compared with 45 per cent of formal and mixed teachers agreed, but over 50 per cent of the latter disagreed, and, somewhat surprisingly, 41 per cent of informal teachers disagreed. That four out of ten informal teachers feel this way when their teaching supposedly capitalises on pupil choice and discovery methods is difficult to explain.

OPINIONS ABOUT TEACHING METHODS

The final section on opinions concerning teaching methods is the most complex, but the most relevant when considering the relationship between opinion and practice. It will be remembered that teachers rated each of ten statements in relation to formal and informal methods. The responses for informal, mixed and formal teachers are shown in table 4.6 and the responses for all teachers are included in appendix B.

The responses of informal, mixed and formal teachers to each statement are presented graphically to afford ease of comprehension.

There is a clear tendency for formal and mixed teachers to disagree with the statement that formal methods create discipline problems, this view being more firmly held by formal teachers. Informal teachers are split on this issue, a similar percentage agreeing and disagreeing. It is interesting to note that although one quarter of informal teachers disagree that informal methods could create discipline problems, nearly 60 per cent agree. In

	Informal — Formal methods					Informal — Informal methods					Formal — Formal methods					Formal — Informal methods					Mixed — Formal methods					Mixed — Informal methods				
	SD	D	N	A	SA	SD	D	N	A	SA	SD	D	N	A	SA	SD	D	N	A	SA	SD	D	N	A	SA	SD	D	N	A	SA
1	8	37	10	38	7	9	25	5	56	7	17	60	8	15	0	0	9	6	74	13	18	55	6	21	0	2	12	7	67	10
2	5	35	5	46	11	14	65	3	17	2	17	56	9	19	0	4	35	20	35	7	11	52	11	25	1	3	52	16	21	18
3	19	54	10	16	2	0	5	3	41	52	7	29	19	36	9	3	2	7	42	48	8	41	10	34	6	3	15	2	41	51
4	20	48	18	15	0	0	5	7	56	33	0	17	23	58	3	3	25	22	49	3	4	6	22	61	7	3	51	16	22	10
5	2	23	6	64	5	0	17	10	67	6	23	65	11	2	0	13	49	25	14	0	1	60	4	7	28	5	17	17	31	1
6	3	52	23	21	3	0	65	12	26	0	25	67	6	3	0	3	14	13	59	13	19	75	10	5	0	1	17	10	53	15
7	8	64	12	15	2	0	50	11	38	0	0	9	26	51	16	2	7	11	59	22	17	31	3	42	7	1	14	6	61	18
8	14	47	15	23	0	0	0	5	66	20	0	9	26	59	0	2	39	39	22	0	5	28	19	42	13	2	30	30	34	43
9	22	56	10	14	0	0	7	10	56	29	2	22	16	59	5	3	37	27	34	2	19	23	19	38	8	3	24	24	46	2
10	29	48	11	13	0	0	5	10	43	44	2	22	25	49	5	0	10	21	64	6	7	26	23	36	7	1	6	20	62	9

SD = Strongly disagree
D = Disagree
N = No opinion
A = Agree
SA = Strongly agree

1 Could create discipline problems
2 Fail to bring the best out of bright pupils
3 Make heavy demands on the teacher
4 Teach basic skills and concepts effectively
5 Encourage time wasting or day dreaming
6 Leave many pupils unsure of what to do
7 Provide the right balance between teaching and individual work
8 Allow each child to develop his full potential
9 Teach pupils to think for themselves

Table 4.6 *Opinions about teaching methods by teaching style*

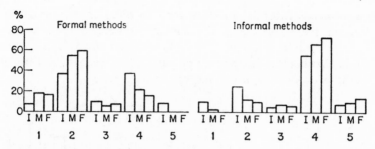

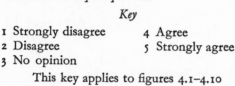

Figure 4.1 *Could create discipline problems*

Key

1 Strongly disagree	4 Agree
2 Disagree	5 Strongly agree
3 No opinion	

This key applies to figures 4.1–4.10

other words they concede that discipline problems could result from the way they teach. As might be expected the vast majority of mixed and formal teachers agree with the statement in relation to informal methods, the formal teachers again holding the strongest views.

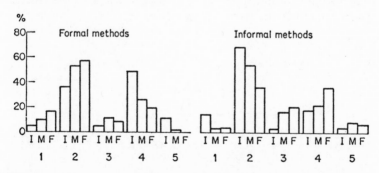

Figure 4.2 *Fail to bring the best out of bright pupils*

Formal teachers and, to a smaller extent, mixed teachers are clear in their denial of the statement in relation to formal methods, and as with the previous statement the informal teachers' opinions are split, 57 per cent agreeing or strongly agreeing that formal methods do fail to bring the best out of bright pupils.

Nevertheless informal teachers tend to disagree that informal methods fail in this way, whereas formal and mixed teachers tend to be split on this issue, with a slight tendency towards disagreement. In other words many are prepared to concede that informal methods do not fail in this respect.

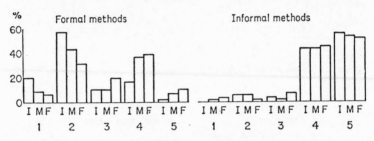

Figure 4.3 *Make heavy demands on the teacher*

On statement 3 there is no doubt in all teachers' minds that informal methods do make a heavy demand on the teacher, but not all formal and mixed teachers are prepared to accept that formal methods do. 45 per cent of formal, and 40 per cent of mixed teachers are of the view that formal methods make the same level of demand. Most informal teachers on the other hand clearly feel that formal methods are easier in this respect.

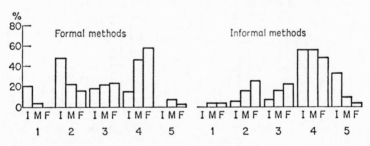

Figure 4.4 *Encourage responsibility and self-discipline*

The encouragement of responsibility and self-discipline was mentioned by a number of informal teachers in the initial interviews and is often seen as a major aim in books reflecting the child centred view of education. There is certainly massive agreement on this from informal teachers, 89 per cent of whom endorse the statement, one-third of the responses being in the 'strongly agree' categoiy. Formal and mixed teachers are less convinced, a bare majority conceding the point.

The interesting feature of responses in relation to formal methods is the relatively high proportion of 'no opinion' statements, almost one in five irrespective of teaching style. Nevertheless a majority of formal and mixed teachers defend the faith whilst the majority of informal teachers feel that formal methods do not perform the function in question.

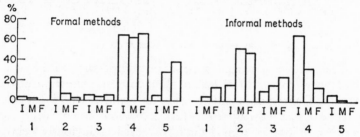

Figure 4.5 *Teach basic skills and concepts effectively*

The large majority of teachers, irrespective of teaching style, believe that formal methods do indeed teach basic skills and concepts effectively. Opinions are split in relation to informal methods, the majority of informal teachers agreeing that informal methods are also effective in this area, and the majority of formal and mixed teachers being more sceptical of such a claim.

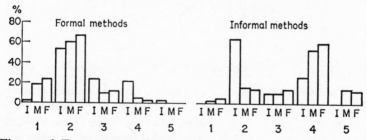

Figure 4.6 *Encourage time wasting or day dreaming*

Again the majority of teachers are prepared to accept that formal methods do not encourage time wasting or day dreaming, and again opinion is divided with respect to informal methods.

The majority of informal teachers do not agree that their methods are guilty of this whilst the majority of formal and mixed teachers point an accusing finger.

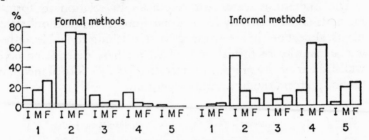

Figure 4.7 *Leave many pupils unsure of what to do*

This statement relates to structure and pertains to the worry that many children feel lost or ill at ease in a situation of free choice. The response pattern is almost identical to that for statement 6 in that most agree that formal methods do not create such a situation whereas formal and mixed teachers obviously feel that informal methods do, leaving informal teachers to defend their practices.

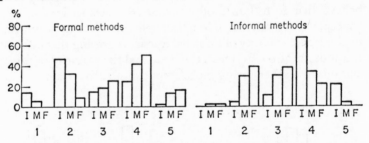

Figure 4.8 *Provide the right balance between teaching and individual work*

The response pattern to this item provides the clearest cleavage between informal, mixed and formal teachers. If the 'strongly disagree' and 'disagree' categories, and the 'agree' and 'strongly agree' categories, are combined then for formal methods the ratio of informal teachers is sixty 'disagree' to twenty-five 'agree', for mixed, thirty-six to fifty-five, and for formal, nine to sixty-seven. For informal methods the ratios are five to eighty-six, thirty-two to thirty-seven, and forty-one to twenty-two. Many teachers apparently could not pass an opinion, most noticeably among formal and mixed teachers.

In general, the majority of informal teachers feel that formal methods do not create the right balance, whilst mixed and formal teachers feel that they do. Informal teachers clearly feel that informal methods provide this balance whilst mixed teachers are not sure, and formal teachers tend to disagree although nearly 40 per cent failed to pass an opinion.

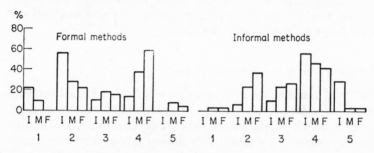

Figure 4.9 *Allow each child to develop his full potential*

A clear difference of opinion occurs with regard to the effi ciency of formal methods in allowing pupils to develop their full potential. Informal teachers dispute the case, formal teachers defend the case, and mixed teachers are uncertain. There is more agreement with the statement in relation to informal methods, the majority conceding the case although 64 per cent of formal teachers either disagree or fail to pass an opinion. Informal teachers are in no doubt, 85 per cent agreeing with the statement.

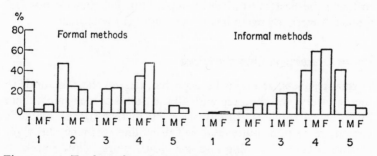

Figure 4.10 *Teach pupils to think for themselves*

Finally, another major objective of informal methods: teaching pupils to think for themselves. Most teachers agree that informal methods do inculcate this skill in their pupils. Informal teachers, as might be expected, most strongly endorse the statement, 44 per cent strongly agreeing. On the other hand informal teachers do not believe that formal methods provide such skills, a point on which formal teachers, and to a lesser extent mixed teachers, do not concur.

A thumb-nail sketch of the views of informal, mixed and formal teachers on informal and formal teaching methods can now be presented by way of summary.

Informal teachers on formal methods

Informal teachers are prepared to concede that formal methods teach basic skills and concepts effectively and provide an environment in which pupils are not unaware of what to do, whilst minimising time wasting and day dreaming. There is however some disagreement among them about the proneness of formal methods to discipline problems. 45 per cent feel that discipline problems could be created under such teaching and another 45 per cent were of the opinion that this is not likely.

Nevertheless they are antipathetic to formal teaching methods on a number of grounds. They feel that such methods fail to encourage responsibility and self-discipline, fail to provide the right balance between teaching and individual work, do not allow the pupils to develop to their full potential, do not teach pupils to think for themselves and, though with less certainty, that they fail to bring the best out in bright pupils. Finally, they do not feel that such methods make heavy demands on the teacher.

Formal teachers on formal methods

Formal teachers, as might be expected, defend their methods in their entirety, and disagree with all the points made against them by informal teachers. Briefly, they claim that formal methods encourage responsibility and self-discipline, provide the right balance between teaching and individual work, allow pupils to develop their full potential, teach pupils to think for themselves, and bring out the best in bright pupils. The only statement on which there was any ambivalence was that relating to demands made on the teacher: 36 per cent of formal teachers felt that demands were not heavy and 45 per cent believed that they were.

Mixed teachers on formal methods

The opinions of mixed teachers, somewhat neatly, come somewhere between those of formal and informal teachers. An examination of the graphs show that in almost every case the strength of responses are somewhat less than in the case of formal teachers, although in total mixed teachers appear to be more aligned with formal than with informal teachers. This difference in emphasis between formal and mixed teachers can be seen in four of the statements. They disagree with formal teachers that formal methods make a heavy demand on teachers, and there is some ambivalence about whether formal methods provide the right balance between teaching and individual work, whether they allow each child to develop to his full potential, and whether they teach pupils to think for themselves.

Formal teachers on informal methods

Just as informal teachers were prepared to concede some points to formal methods, so formal teachers are prepared to concede some to informal methods. They agree for instance that informal methods are likely to encourage responsibility and self-discipline, and that they teach pupils to think for themselves. They also concur with the view that informal methods make heavy demands on the teacher. However, they feel strongly that informal methods could create discipline problems, that they do not teach basic skills and concepts effectively, that such methods encourage time wasting, and leave pupils unsure of what to do. They are also of the opinion, by a much smaller margin, that informal methods fail to provide the right balance between teaching and individual work, do not allow each child to develop to his full potential, and, again marginally, that these methods fail to bring out the best in bright pupils.

Informal teachers on informal methods

Formal teachers were not prepared to concede any points against formal methods and this is repeated in this instance, with the exception of discipline. Almost two thirds of informal teachers agreed that informal methods could indeed create discipline problems. On every other statement there is a clear majority in the expected direction.

Mixed teachers on informal methods

Mixed teachers' views on informal methods again come somewhere between those of informal and formal teachers. They agree that informal methods teach pupils to think for themselves, encourage responsibility and self-discipline and make heavy demands on the teacher. They disagree with the formal teachers' evaluation of informal methods on two statements: they agree, marginally in both cases, that informal methods provide the right balance between teaching and individual work, and allow each child to develop to his full potential. They agree with formal teachers, though with less emphasis in each case, that informal methods could create discipline problems, fail to bring the best out of bright pupils, do not teach basic skills effectively, encourage time wasting, and leave pupils unsure of what to do.

Asking teachers to pass judgements on aspects of both formal and informal methods has proved to be a fruitful mode of inquiry. Both informal and formal teachers were effective counsels for the defence of their own methods and probing prosecuting counsels against each other's methods. Mixed teachers were more akin to interested, fairly unconvinced observers.

These analyses represent one step forward from Ashton's analyses, and confirm that opinions about teaching methods are firmly held and that, in general, opinions relate strongly to classroom practice.

5

Pupil progress

Too often in the past researchers have adopted a one-shot testing programme when attempting to attribute differential effects on pupils to different teaching styles. This is a weak inferential process since analyses of change or progress are not possible. To answer the question 'Do teaching styles result in differential pupil progress?' requires a research design which allows for a follow up of samples of pupils over an extended period of time during which they experience differing teaching approaches. By testing at the beginning and end of this period, progress can be assessed and differential effects, if any, established.

A quasi-experimental design was adopted which is shown diagramatically in figure 5.1. The first stage involved the selection of thirty-seven teachers to represent seven of the twelve types isolated in the teacher typology. These seven were chosen since they represented the whole range, and could be collapsed into three general styles, informal, mixed and formal. Types 1 and 2 represented informal styles, 3, 4 and 7 represented mixed styles, and 11 and 12 formal styles. It should not be thought that by choosing styles 3, 4 and 7 to represent mixed teaching approaches a bias towards informal styles was built in. The clear continuum implied by the diagrammatic representation in figure 5.1 is an over-simplification of a highly complex pattern.

Twelve teachers were initially chosen to represent each style, six each from types 1, 2, 11 and 12, and four each from types 3, 4 and 7, but an additional teacher was added to the informal sample because of the small size of one informal classroom. The teachers selected were in each case those whose profiles most closely matched the group profile of their parent type, in other words those teachers who most closely matched the relevant type-description presented in chapter 3. This selection procedure

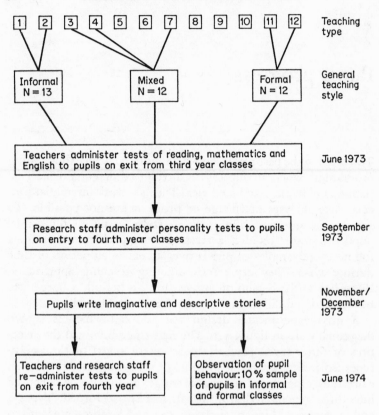

Figure 5.1 *Simplified sampling and research design*

gave a pupil sample of approximately 400 per general teaching style.

It was decided that the teachers themselves should administer the attainment tests under normal classroom conditions, to obviate a test atmosphere and, hopefully, to reduce anxiety. The first administration was carried out by third-year teachers who were provided with detailed instructions by the research team. The personality tests were administered by the research team within one month of the pupils' entry into their new fourth-year classes. These same attainment and personality tests were re-administered the following June in the same manner.

In addition to the standardised attainment tests two examples of written work were taken towards the end of the autumn term, the results of which are presented in chapter 7.

Analysis of change

In educational experiments it is rarely if ever possible to allocate pupils to treatments randomly, and as a consequence the average scores of the samples at the pre-test stage could be disparate. In this instance the pupils in the formal sample had higher scores on the three attainment tests. A statistical analysis was therefore required which took differences in initial achievement into account. Analysis of covariance was chosen following the practice adopted in similar types of study, e.g. those of Soar and Barker Lunn. Such an analysis is preferable to the use of raw gain scores, i.e. post-test scores minus pre-test scores, since these suffer from the fact that the unreliability in both pre- and post-test scores are combined. Neither do they take into account differences in initial achievement.

Details of sampling and the analysis of covariance tables are presented in appendix C. They show that in each attainment area the effect of teaching style is highly significant, although the effect of initial level of achievement is most powerful. Residual gain scores were then computed for each type of attainment separately. These scores are interpreted as the difference between observed and predicted scores: i.e. did pupils exposed to the three general teaching styles progress as well as, better than, or worse than would have been expected on the basis of their level of initial achievement?

READING

It is apposite to consider reading first, in the light of the recent publication of the Bullock Report (1975) *A Language for Life*. However, a clarification of terminology is necessary because Bullock uses the term 'teaching method' to refer to specific approaches to the teaching of reading such as 'look and say' and phonics. Teaching style as defined in this study corresponds more closely with what the report calls 'school organisation', although this latter term is probably less satisfactory since it contains the implied assumption that schools as a whole follow certain teaching practices, whereas in reality classes within the same school are often organised very differently.

In discussing the relationship between teaching styles and the development of reading the report reiterates the argument contained in chapter 1, noting the uninformed nature of the public debate and the tendency to generalise on the basis of extreme forms of teaching. It noted that this is an area where personal impression counts heavily, a point epitomised by the note of dissension on the part of Froome, who asserted that creativity is reverenced and formal work virtually banished in schools today, neither of which are borne out by the present study, or by the survey contained within the Bullock Report itself. Nevertheless the report did criticise some aspects of informal teaching. Forms of integrated day which used assignment cards came under fire, since these made possible no interpretation of language or other learning experiences and provided children with little contact with the teacher. Although the impression was created that children had choice of topic and were working at their own pace, the work was as narrow as or narrower than the more formal variety it replaced. It was also reported that members of the committee had talked to teachers who felt it wrong to teach the class as a whole directly since this would compromise their commitment to a child centred programme. The members felt that such extremes could not be justified since the degree of structure and the mode of learning differs from one situation to another, and the teacher's repertoire of methods of organisation should be able to accommodate these various needs.

On the basis of their deliberations the committee felt able to prescribe a 'best buy'. It was claimed that

independent work, by individuals and groups, provides the best sustained context for effective instruction by the teacher and should therefore be the principal form of classroom activity. There will be some occasions when the teacher will find it appropriate to teach the whole class, or when the whole class will be watching and listening to something collectively. When an organisation of this flexible kind is working successfully, frequent and regular timetable breaks are likely to amount to an interruption of learning.

The report appears to eschew formal and informal teaching styles in favour of what in this study are termed mixed styles. However, it might be thought paradoxical that only a few paragraphs earlier in the report a call had been made for serious study of the conditions in which children learn most efficiently, with the rider that 'in our view it is naive to believe that a particular form of organisation will in itself guarantee them'. Whether mixed styles do provide the greatest progress in reading, as Bullock and Soar would appear to suggest, can now be assessed.

Results

The Bullock committee were concerned that the reading tests widely used were assessing only a narrow range of reading abilities, and advocated an instrument that combined practicality with a more comprehensive and therefore more realistic sampling of skills. This accorded with our own thinking, and, after a survey of available tests, the Edinburgh Reading Test Stage III (Moray House) was chosen. This covered the required age range, 10 years to 12 years 6 months, without creating a ceiling effect, and at the same time sampled five different reading abilities: reading for facts; comprehension of sequences; retention of main ideas; comprehension of points of view; and vocabulary.

The 'reading for facts' section was designed to sample some of the processes involved in the type of reading used in referring to books and other sources of information, for example in connection with project work. In this the reader has to examine various parts of the material in search of relevant information; he has to disregard what is not relevant and hold some parts in mind as potentially helpful whilst he seeks for further evidence. The reader has to translate statements into other words and to make inferences from the given data in coming to decisions as to the categories into which he will place the statements. To reach the conclusion that a statement is false requires the recognition of statements to the contrary. Success in this section requires a clear understanding of what the passage says and ability to examine the evidence carefully.

'Comprehension of sequences' assesses the pupil's ability to comprehend sequences of events, as in narrative material, or to follow the steps in a piece of reasoning. From a variety of seman-tic and structural clues within each sentence the pupil has to organise the sentences in such a way as to form a consistent se-quence. It is believed that the skills tested in this section are significant for competent reading.

The intention of the 'retention of main ideas' section is to assess the child's ability to learn through reading as he would be called upon to do in individual study. He is asked to decide what the main ideas in the passage are and to reproduce them in a recognition situation within a very short time. In other words this section deals with recall.

'Comprehension of points of view' assesses the extent to which the child is capable of building up clusters of ideas which repre-sent different points of view on topics which could be classified as mildly controversial. In order to match the statements with the characters participating in the discussion outlined in the passage, a thorough assimilation of what is said in the passage is necessary. This process of matching calls for the translation of material into other words, and the making of inferences.

Finally, the 'vocabulary' section assesses the extent of the child's familiarity with the meanings of words and phrases. Deficiencies in vocabulary set limits to competence in all types of reading, and the extension of knowledge of meanings of words is essen-tial if progress in reading is to be maintained.

Differential gain on progress in reading in relation to teaching style is shown in figure 5.2. The scores represent the average

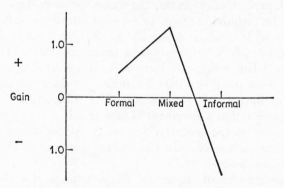

Figure 5.2 *Differential gain in reading by teaching style*

Reading						
	Formal		Mixed		Informal	
Initial achievement	Boys	Girls	Boys	Girls	Boys	Girls
80–	81·3 [12]	91·1 [8]	89·3 [25]	91·3 [24]	87·8 [24]	85·5 [20]
80–89	92·4 [24]	94·5 [17]	92·9 [29]	94·5 [35]	95·7 [29]	94·5 [32]
90–99	101·5 [39]	101·1 [30]	104·1 [33]	100·8 [28]	99·5 [30]	97·1 [39]
100–109	111·9 [41]	110·5 [51]	110·8 [27]	109·9 [27]	108·3 [32]	108·6 [38]
110–119	119·4 [29]	117·8 [29]	120·7 [17]	118·0 [22]	113·2 [20]	118·0 [21]
120+	127·0 [29]	125·4 [26]	127·2 [15]	126·7 [12]	120·7 [17]	123·8 [19]

Table 5.1 *Post-test achievement in reading by initial level of achievement, sex and teaching style*

gain or loss over the school year above or below that predicted from initial achievement. If progress has occurred at the predicted rate the score is zero, if progress is better than predicted the score is positive, and if less than expected, negative. It should be noted that a negative score does not indicate that ground has actually been lost, only that progress has not been made at the level expected.

Children in mixed classes show the greatest overall gain although the difference between mixed and formal is not significant. The differences between mixed and informal, and formal and informal, are both highly significant, however. It is clear that overall progress in informal classrooms is significantly inferior to that in mixed and formal classrooms.

Further analyses were carried out to assess whether this general picture was true across all achievement levels and to examine whether progress for boys and girls exhibited a similar pattern. The results are shown in table 5.1 and figures 5.3 and 5.4.

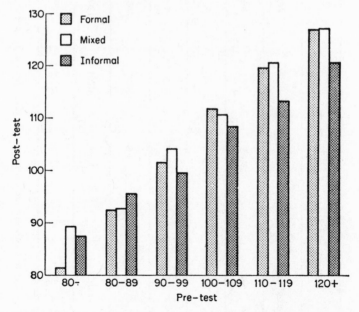

Figure 5.3 *Post-test achievement by initial level of achievement in reading — boys*

The table and figures show the post-test achievement of boys at six levels of initial achievement. It would seem that mixed and informal teaching styles are more effective for the lower achieving boys, particularly in the 80− group. Beyond a reading quotient of 100, however, the mixed and formal boys exhibit superior progress. Among boys of reading quotient 110+ this lead stretches to some six or seven points, equivalent to something in the order of nine months' discrepancy in reading age.

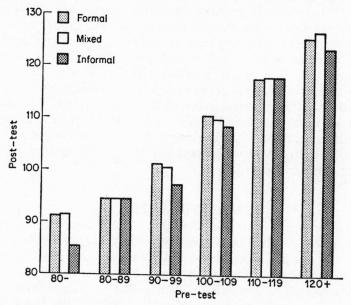

Figure 5.4 *Post-test achievement by initial level of achievement in reading – girls*

This ineffectiveness of formal teaching among low achieving boys does not appear among low achieving girls. In fact the reverse situation occurs, formal and mixed pupils showing a marked superiority in progress over informal girls (figure 5.4). Few differences between mixed and formal teaching occur throughout the remainder of the achievement levels, but informally taught girls lag somewhat behind.

There are only minor sex differences, the only significant one being that between boys and girls in the 80− range in formal classes. The overall trend among formal and mixed pupils is for the girls to perform slightly less well than the boys, whereas among informal pupils the girls tend to progress less well in the lower achievement levels, and slightly better in the higher levels.

Summary

The results provide clear evidence for the better performance of formal and mixed pupils in reading progress. The findings are statistically and educationally significant, showing the equivalent of some three to five months' difference in reading age.

The effect is more apparent among boys, particularly among those with a quotient above 100 where the discrepancies between formal and informal and mixed and informal stretch to some six or seven points. Nevertheless there is also evidence to suggest that low achieving boys in formal classes perform less well than those of equivalent achievement in mixed and informal classes. This was only true of boys since formal girls showed better progress than their counterparts in other types of classroom. Few sex differences emerged.

MATHEMATICS

The Plowden Report contrasted the old and the new in primary mathematics. 'Until comparatively recently a typical "scheme of work" in a primary school could have been summarised somewhat as follows: "Composition and decomposition of 10. The four rules. The four rules in money. Tables. Vulgar fractions. Simple decimals. Simple problems." Emphasis was laid upon knowledge of tables, computation and quick and accurate "mental arithmetic".' The writers of the report perceived that change had occurred since the early 1950s and that during the sixties 'new ideas have spread so as to affect at least a majority of primary schools, and to justify the name of revolution in a substantial minority.'

The Schools Council Curriculum Bulletin No 1 is quoted as summarising these new ideas:

1 Children learn mathematical concepts more slowly than we realised. They learn by their own activities.

2 Although children think and reason in different ways they all pass

through certain stages depending on their chronological and mental ages and their experience.

3 We can accelerate their learning by providing suitable experiences, particularly if we introduce the appropriate language simultaneously.

4 Practice is necessary to fix a concept once it has been understood, therefore practice should follow, and not precede, discovery.

The practical consequences of these principles, argued the report, is that instead of being presented with ready-made problems in a textbook the children find their own problems or are given them in a 'raw form', with the aim of their learning a mathematical concept. Thus the situation becomes more relevant. Nevertheless, they also point out that this does not remove the necessity for a carefully thought out scheme of work, for careful individual records of progress and for practice in computation and accuracy. It was acknowledged that this would require a greater degree of understanding on the part of the teacher, but concluded that 'there is ample evidence that many of the claims made for the new approach are well founded', and that 'it is desirable that this development should continue.' As usual no evidence is cited in support of such claims. The argument for the efficiency of activity based teaching approaches can now be assessed.

Results

It has been argued that conventional attainment tests are less valid for the assessment of the new than the old maths. A test was therefore chosen which, in the words of the publisher, is 'broader in content than traditional arithmetic tests'. The Mathematics Attainment Test (DE2, N.F.E.R.) was designed to assess mathematical understanding rather than skill in computation. A proportion of the time taken by a child to complete the test is therefore 'thinking time'.

The results of the analysis relating gain in mathematics to teaching style are presented in graphical form in figure 5.5 overleaf.

The pattern here is different from that of reading. Children in formal classes still exhibit substantial progress but this is not so for those in mixed and informal classes. The differences between formal styles on the one hand, and mixed and informal styles on

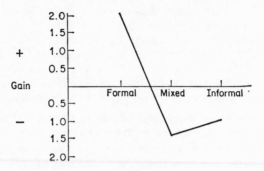

Figure 5.5 *Gain in mathematics by teaching style*

the other are highly significant, being equivalent to some four or five months' differential progress.

Post-test scores were computed for six levels of initial achievement, sex and teaching styles and are presented in table 5.2 and figures 5.6 and 5.7.

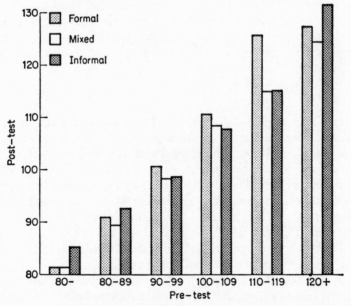

Figure 5.6 *Post-test achievement by level of initial achievement in mathematics – boys*

Mathematics	Formal		Mixed		Informal	
Initial achievement	Boys	Girls	Boys	Girls	Boys	Girls
80–	81.4 [12]	90.0 [3]	81.4 [13]	82.9 [15]	85.3 [11]	82.0 [10]
80–89	91.0 [26]	90.0 [20]	89.4 [46]	87.7 [31]	92.9 [31]	89.4 [32]
90–99	100.8 [31]	103.0 [44]	98.3 [31]	97.8 [54]	98.9 [38]	96.3 [54]
100–109	110.2 [60]	111.3 [53]	108.2 [34]	107.2 [27]	107.9 [50]	107.3 [45]
110–119	125.8 [26]	120.0 [27]	115.0 [14]	119.6 [16]	115.1 [18]	118.9 [20]
120+	127.4 [19]	130.6 [14]	124.6 [8]	123.8 [5]	131.8 [4]	125.8 [8]

Table 5.2 Post-test achievement in mathematics by initial level of achievement, sex and teaching style

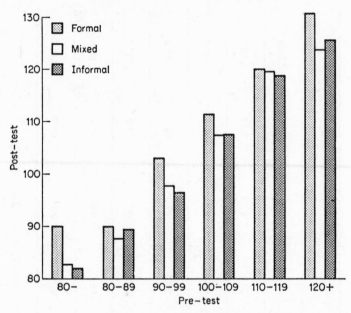

Figure 5.7 *Post-test achievement by initial level of achievement in mathematics – girls*

Above a mathematics quotient of 90 the boys in formal classrooms exhibit greater progress than those in mixed and informal classrooms. The high performance of informal boys of quotient 120+ is difficult to interpret since this group contains only four boys and is thus unlikely to be reliable. The performance of low achievers is again worthy of note under formal teaching, which replicates the pattern found in reading: boys of a low initial achievement level under-achieve, whereas girls of a similar level do not. In fact, girls informal classrooms show superior progress at every level of achievement, most markedly those with a quotient of 120+.

Sex differences are again slight, the only significant difference being between boys and girls in formal classes in the range 110–19.

Summary

Better progress in mathematical understanding is evident with formal teaching styles and is apparent at every level of achievement except among the lowest achieving boys. This superiority tends to increase with level of achievement. It could be surmised that class teaching in formal classrooms may be pitched at a level that is beyond the capabilities of the less able boys. On the other hand concern must also be expressed at the apparent inability of mixed and informal teaching to fulfil the potential of the most able pupils.

ENGLISH

The standard of children's performance in writing and English is a rich source of controversy in educational circles. Secondary school teachers want pupils to enter with a basic grounding in literacy, which includes the skills of spelling, punctuation and grammar, whilst many primary teachers tend to emphasise free or creative writing. There appears to be little or no research examining performance in English by teaching style, but this does not stop assertions that there is a decline in the art of children's written expression. Froome (1974) for example blames the inspectorate for advising teachers that they should not worry children unduly with writing form, spelling, punctuation and grammatical sentence construction. Thus, he claims, their ability to communicate accurately has become stultified by the exuberance of their own creativity.

The move towards free writing was certainly endorsed by the Plowden Report. Spelling, punctuation and comprehension are words not mentioned in their consideration of English, whereas 'free, fluent and copious writing' is given an unqualified welcome. An analysis of all these skills is undertaken in chapter 7. Here the analysis of pupil progress is restricted to a conventional English Progress Test (D3, N.F.E.R.), whose major emphasis is on comprehension but includes punctuation and sentence completion sections.

The basic analysis of pupil gain by teaching style is presented in graphical form in figure 5.8 overleaf.

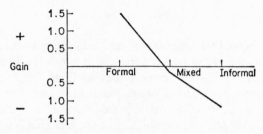

Figure 5.8 *Gains in English by teaching style*

The relationship is almost linear, most progress being made under formal teaching, least under informal teaching, with mixed teaching in between. The difference in progress between formal and informal is slightly less than in mathematics and equivalent to approximately three or four months. The differences between formal and mixed, and between formal and informal, are both statistically significant.

Table 5.3 and figures 5.9 and 5.10 show progress at differing levels of achievement and by sex.

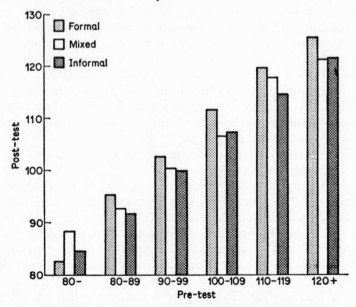

Figure 5.9 *Post-test scores in English by initial achievement level – boys*

Initial achievement level	Formal		Mixed		Informal	
	Boys	Girls	Boys	Girls	Boys	Girls
80–	82.9 [9]	88.0 [4]	88.8 [18]	88.5 [13]	84.9 [16]	85.3 [12]
80–89	96.3 [23]	91.9 [8]	92.8 [31]	92.6 [27]	92.0 [24]	93.0 [21]
90–99	102.7 [37]	100.9 [24]	100.4 [33]	102.5 [43]	100.1 [43]	101.3 [48]
100–109	111.9 [51]	112.8 [48]	106.6 [31]	111.8 [33]	107.3 [41]	108.4 [43]
110–119	119.9 [28]	119.5 [53]	118.0 [25]	115.5 [21]	114.8 [20]	116.0 [24]
120+	125.3 [26]	126.0 [24]	120.5 [8]	121.3 [11]	121.9 [8]	124.5 [21]

Table 5.3 *Final achievement by initial achievement level – English*

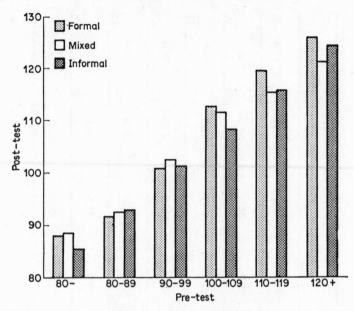

Figure 5.10 *Post-test scores in English by initial achievement level – girls*

Formal boys are superior to mixed and informal boys at every achievement level except the lowest, which reveals once again the under-achievement of this group under formal teaching. Also repeated is the finding that the lowest achieving girls do not share this characteristic. Nevertheless girls with an English quotient below 100 in mixed classes show superior progress to those in formal and informal classrooms. Thereafter formal girls exhibit most progress.

Sex differences are again slight although the trend is for girls to show slightly better progress than boys in this area.

Summary

Overall, pupils in formal classrooms show significantly better progress in English than those in mixed and informal classrooms. Mixed pupils also show significantly better progress than informal pupils.

The formal boys are superior at every achievement level other than the lowest, whilst mixed girls have higher scores below a quotient of 100, beyond which point formal girls show the greatest progress. Sex differences are slight.

CASE STUDY:
A HIGH GAIN INFORMAL CLASSROOM

The results presented so far portray a fairly dismal picture of achievement in informal classrooms. Nevertheless there was one such classroom which was categorised high gain in every achievement area; indeed in one area it was the highest gain class. It was therefore felt important that this class and teacher should be examined more closely. All the information on the class was gathered together from the initial questionnaire, the research team and advisors' ratings, children's stories and observation evidence, and was supplemented by an interview with the teacher. From this information an interesting picture emerged, some parts of which differed from the picture of other informal classes.

The teacher was a woman in her middle thirties with ten years' teaching experience. The school was situated in a new town and the class, according to the teacher, was comprised of pupils with the full range of abilities. She felt she was an informal teacher and was in fact categorised as type 2 in the typology, i.e. not the most informal type. Both the research team and advisors also categorised her as informal, and her aims and opinions expressed in the questionnaire were also very informally orientated.

The first factor which differentiated this teacher from other informal teachers was the amount of time spent on mathematics and English, which was equal to, or in excess of, that spent by many formal classes. In other words, the curriculum emphasis was placed on the cognitive rather than the affective/aesthetic. Standards were set by the head. When she was interviewed about the past year in her school, she stated: 'Whilst there was a lot of emphasis on the social aspects in the school the children are encouraged to be work-minded right from the infants. The idea was not to kill learning but that the children should enjoy what they were doing.' Nevertheless, she was free to choose her own syllabus. 'I used "Metric Maths" and "Beta Maths". We followed the method of beta supplemented by hundreds of work sheets and cards. By the third term the children worked mainly from the work sheets. The metric maths involved reading and comprehension. In the third year the children had done some formal classwork in maths.'

She did not use any set books for English. 'We did a lot of creative writing, stories and topic work. All the grammar stemmed from that. Language and vocabulary work was tackled more individually or in groups. I would deal with things like speech marks when they were needed.'

For reading, the Ward-Lock reading workshop was used. The manual recommends that it should be used for short periods: 'so we used it for two six-week periods'.

The teacher had her own system of records, mainly of attainment, including records of group and individual work, and also of social behaviour. She had also built up a large stock of teaching materials over the years. With reference to incentives she stated that she was the main incentive: 'personality has a lot to do with it: they know I will be pleased if they do well.'

When she was told of the progress of her pupils on the attainment tests she indicated that in the main the results were as she had expected. 'I would be disappointed if a class went out without my feeling that all the children achieved something. The poorer ones perhaps did not improve as much as I would have liked. They seemed to improve particularly with regard to maths. At the beginning of the year they groaned when they were to do maths but by the end of the year they liked it.'

An added factor that may or may not be relevant is that her own daughter, whom she was hoping to get accepted by one of the better known girls' public schools, was one of the pupils.

In the context of open-plan primary schools it has been said by practitioners and advisors alike that successful implementation requires good organisation and a clear structure. This would seem to be exemplified in this classroom. Although the classroom was evidently orientated towards informal practices the content of the curriculum was clearly organised and well structured. This would seem to highlight a distinction between how the learning environment is structured, on the one hand, and the emphasis and structure of curriculum content, on the other. At the risk of introducing yet another ill-defined dichotomy, this distinction could be conceptualised as cognitively orientated informality versus affectively or aesthetically orientated informality, the latter laying greater stress on social and moral development, with less emphasis on content and structure.

EFFECT OF ELEVEN-PLUS

Analyses have so far concentrated on the internal aspects of classroom practice, but as reported in chapter 3, a number of external influences appeared to be operating, the most powerful being the effect of an eleven-plus selective examination. In order to probe more deeply into the relationship between the presence of the selective examination and pupil gain, analyses were carried out contrasting gain of pupils in schools subjected to eleven-plus procedures and in schools that were not. The overall effect is shown in table 5.4.

Gain in	11+	No 11+
English	+0·5	−0·5
Maths	+0·1	−0·8
Reading	+1·7	−1·7
Number of schools	13	24

Table 5.4 *Effect of eleven-plus on pupil gain*

These data would appear to substantiate the claims sometimes made that an examination of this kind tends to support standards in the basic subjects. But the gain scores in this table are confounded by the fact that very few informal schools were in selective areas. Analyses of differential gain within teaching style

Gain in	11+	No 11+
English	+1·5	+1·6
Maths	+1·8	+1·0
Reading	+0·9	−0·7
Number of schools	5	7

Table 5.5 *Gain in formal schools in selective and non-selective areas*

were therefore computed and are presented in tables 5.5, 5.6 and
5.7. Five of the twelve formal schools were in selective areas and
from table 5.5 it can be seen that only in maths and reading is
there a differential effect, the more noticeable being in reading.
Nevertheless, in general, pupils in formal classes in selective areas
progress more than pupils in formal classes in non-selective areas.

The findings are not as clear cut in mixed schools although
again superior progress in reading is apparent in eleven-plus
classes. There is little difference in mathematics, but in English,
pupils in eleven-plus classes progress less than those in non-
eleven-plus classes.

Gain in	11+	No 11+
English	−1·2	−0·4
Maths	−2·0	−2·3
Reading	+1·2	−1·3
Number of schools	5	7

Table 5.6 *Gain in mixed schools in selective and non-selective areas*

The results from informal schools should be treated with cau-
tion since only three of the schools were in a selective area. Nevertheless, the pattern is unequivocal and the differences, apart
from those in maths, are massive.

Gain in	11+	No 11+
English	+1·6	−2·2
Maths	−0·4	−1·0
Reading	+4·4	−3·0
Number of schools	3	10

Table 5.7 *Gain in informal schools in selective and non-selective areas*

There is a certain logic to these results if the argument is
accepted that external conditions placed upon informal classes
do not alter teaching and organisation but necessitate a greater
emphasis on the cognitive than on the affective domain. In other
words, informal classes could be cognitively orientated, stressing

basic skills at the expense of aesthetic activities, or vice versa. At this stage this reasoning is conjectural, but it accords with experience.

With the exception of selective mixed schools the eleven-plus would seem to relate to greater cognitive growth, particularly in reading, and most noticeably in informal schools.

GENERAL SUMMARY

Reading

1 Pupils taught by formal and mixed styles show significantly superior progress as compared with those taught by informal styles.

2 The effect is more noticeable in average and above average achievers. Low achieving boys in formal classrooms progress less well than expected, but this is not true of low achieving formal girls. Above average boys in informal classrooms markedly under-achieve in comparison to boys of the same ability in mixed and formal classrooms.

Mathematics

1 Pupils taught by formal styles show significantly superior progress to that of those taught by mixed and informal styles.

2 The superiority exists at every level of achievement among boys and girls, with the exception of the least able boys, who again progress less well than expected.

English

1 Pupils taught by formal styles show significantly superior progress as compared with those taught by mixed and informal styles. Mixed pupils also show progress significantly superior to that of informal pupils.

2 Formal boys gain higher scores at every level of achievement, with the exception of the least able. Mixed girls progress most below an English quotient of 100, beyond which formal girls show greatest progress.

Eleven-plus

The presence of a selective examination at the age of eleven is related to superior progress, particularly in reading, and most noticeably in informal classrooms.

High gain informal classroom

The most noticeable features of this classroom were the juxta-position of informal classroom organisation with a clear curriculum structure, and emphasis upon cognitive rather than affective/aesthetic content.

6

Observation of pupil behaviour

Although it would seem that formal teaching styles engender in their pupils greater progress in the basic subjects, there is as yet no information which casts light on why this should be. What mechanisms within the on-going classroom situation are instrumental in such growth? Evidence of this nature was gathered during the observational stage of the study.

It was decided to focus the observation on pupils rather than teachers. This decision was taken partly in the light of Carroll's (1963) model of school learning in which he holds that one of the crucial factors in attainment gain is the use made by pupils of the opportunities provided by teachers. Indeed one of the clearest findings from the few studies which have observed pupil behaviour is the relationship between work involvement or task attention and cognitive growth (Lahaderne 1968; Cobb 1972; Samuels and Turnure 1974; McKinney and others 1975). It is now becoming recognised that focusing on dimensions of pupil behaviour will probably reveal far more about the effectiveness of teaching than directly studying the teacher.

The observation was designed to meet two objectives, firstly to investigate the classroom behaviour of pupils in relation to differences in teaching style; and second, to observe pupils of different personality type in order to assess the relationship between pupils' responses to paper and pencil personality tests and their actual classroom behaviour. The first objective is the concern of this chapter; the second will be examined in chapter 8.

A suitable observational instrument was not available, so it was necessary to develop what came to be called the Pupil Behaviour Inventory (Wade 1976).

The first stage in the development of the P.B.I. involved the collection of pupil behaviour items, and for this purpose visits were made to three different types of classroom as classified by teacher questionnaire responses. All pupils in these classrooms were observed for short periods, and their behaviours listed. Subsequently items of behaviour were sorted into categories. The categories decided upon were:

1 Work activity
Sub-categories included under this heading were:

(a) *Preparation:* behaviours such as getting or putting away materials

(b) *Miscellaneous:* activities involved here are those which are not classified under other headings – ruling lines, consulting charts and other activities of this nature

(c) *Writing:* all writing activities from copying to essay writing or note taking

(d) *Computation:* any work activity involving mathematics

(e) *Making:* all constructive or art work

(f) *Reading:* time actually spent reading or consulting book

(g) *Waiting:* queueing to see teacher etc.

2 Interaction
It was decided that interaction with peers should be recorded separately from interaction with the teacher. The following sub-categories were included:

(a) *Asking:* all pupil questioning that is work related

(b) *Responding:* work-related responses

(c) *Cooperating:* all activities that involve cooperation with work or sharing of materials

(d) *Play:* non-work-related interaction that is friendly in character – chatting or passing messages

(e) *Attracting attention:* items such as nudging, making signs

(f) *Negative/disputative:* behaviour of an anti-social nature

3 Other activity
Other categories deemed to be of interest were:

(a) *Watching:* (i) pupil directed: behaviours such as standing up to look at another, sitting, watching; (ii) teacher directed: glancing round at the teacher

(b) *Avoidance:* items here included gazing into space, looking out of the window, doing nothing or not answering when spoken to

4 Movement
(a) *Fidget:* a long list of items was included here such as scratching, shuffling, playing with hair or pencil, tapping and rocking on the chair
(b) *Classroom:* includes all activities which involve pupils leaving their places

A preliminary schedule was devised on the basis of these categories, a pilot study on one hundred pupils carried out, and minor modifications made. The final schedule is presented in Wade (1976). Inter-observer reliabilities have been ascertained to be in excess of 0·8 after eight hours' training. In other words, there is a high degree of agreement between observers on the recording of pupil behaviours.

Sample

It had been intended to observe a 15 per cent sample of all pupils in formal and informal classrooms. The sampling procedure itself was designed to facilitate the second of the objectives, to discover the relationship between classroom behaviour and personality profiles. In order to implement this a cluster analysis was carried out to group together pupils who had similar personality characteristics. Eight pupil personality types were indicated and it was from these that the observation sample was drawn.

Unfortunately some diminution of sample size occurred because of factors beyond the control of the research team. In two instances a supply teacher had taken over the class for a short period whilst the class teacher was in one instance attending a short course, and in the other taking an examination. Since the teaching style of the supply teacher was unknown it was decided to drop these classrooms from the analysis. Losses also occurred because of absence from school during the observation period. Ultimately a total of 101 pupils were observed, fifty-three in informal classes, and forty-eight in formal classes. The fact that the sample was drawn from the typology, combined with sample loss, served to provide a sample that was not representative of the whole sample in terms of achievement. To alleviate this the sample was split into high, average and low achievers by dividing the distribution of initial achievement at the 33rd and 66th percentile. This resulted in thirty-two high, thirty-four average and thirty-five low achievers.

Method

The procedure adopted was that of observing each child for ten five minute periods. Children were observed in rotation. During each five minute period five second counts were made, at the end of which all behaviour was recorded in the form of tallies. All listed behaviours were recorded so that if, for example, a child was observed to fidget whilst writing, two tallies were made. This method was adopted for two reasons:

1 The observer was not required to decide which item of behaviour was more important
2 It enabled the collection of more information within a limited time period

On entering the classroom the observer was introduced by the teachers concerned as a visitor who had 'come to watch for a day like the students do'. A seating plan was then drawn up by the observer on which the teacher could place the children without their being aware of the observer's focus. Subsequently the observer chose a quiet vantage point which enabled maximum view of all the subjects.

Scoring

Work-related activity

By adding the number of tallies in the seven categories included under this heading a frequency count was obtained for total work. Since it was felt that in some cases considerable time was wasted by pupils in protracted preparation activities, and in waiting to see the teacher, it was decided to subtract the sum of these two categories from the total work count to give an actual work count.

Pupil interaction

A frequency count of pupil interaction was obtained by summing the six categories of behaviour included under this heading. A further summation of the categories of asking, responding and cooperative behaviour was made to give a work-related interaction sub-total. The remaining categories of attracting attention, play/chat and negative/argumentative behaviour were also summed to give a frequency count of social or non-work-related interaction.

Teacher interaction

As teacher-related interaction behaviours were found to occur much less frequently than other categories of behaviour these were all summed to give a total teacher-interaction count.

Non-work-related activities

The remaining observed activities were totalled separately, as these were behaviours which could be tallied concurrently. Thus separate totals were retained for the categories of fidgeting, classroom movement, avoidance, watching pupils and watching teacher.

Analyses

Since frequency counts of behaviour were the outcome of the observation, non-parametric statistics were used for the analysis. Mann-Whitney U tests were thus carried out on each of the thirty-one behaviour variables.

Work activity

Figure 6.1 (and tables 1, 2 and 3 in appendix D) shows the median scores for total work activity for the three achievement levels. High achieving formal pupils engage in significantly more work activity than their informal counterparts, and when preparation time is deducted to give an actual work activity score the

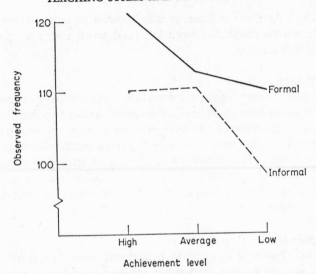

Figure 6.1 *Median scores for total work activity for three achievement levels in formal and informal classrooms*

differences are even greater (figure 6.2). In fact the actual work engaged in by high achieving informal pupils is considerably lower than the average for all pupils and is no greater than that for low achieving informal pupils. The large discrepancies between high achieving formal and informal pupils are due to the higher incidence of work on writing, computation and making by formal pupils, plus the fact that they spend far less time on preparation activities.

Among average achieving pupils there is little difference in actual work activity, but among low achievers those in formal classrooms again engage in significantly more work activity.

Pupils in formal classrooms engage in more work related activity, irrespective of level of initial achievement, the discrepancies being particularly large at high and low achievement levels.

Work related interaction (Figure 6.3 and tables 4, 5 and 6 in appendix D)

Some explanation of the low levels of actual work in informal classrooms is presented here, where it can be seen that, except

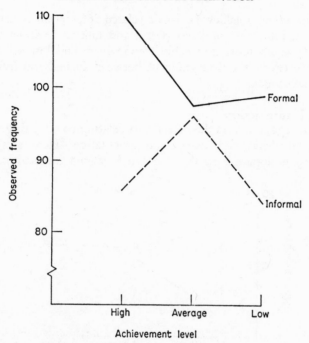

Figure 6.2 *Median scores for actual work activity for three achievement levels in formal and informal classrooms*

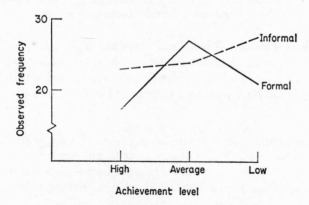

Figure 6.3 *Median scores for work-related pupil interaction for three achievement levels in formal and informal classrooms*

among average achievers, work related interaction is higher.* That is, informal pupils cooperate and talk more about work. This is again most noticeable among high and low achievers, but the effect is only significant between formal and informal high achievers.

Social interaction

This category covers the behaviours relating to attracting attention, play/chat and negative/argumentative. Here a similar pattern is apparent to that for work related interaction. The

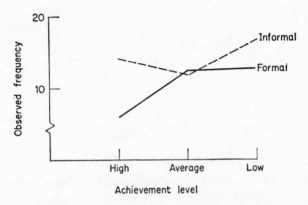

Figure 6.4 *Median scores for social pupil interaction for three achievement levels in formal and informal classrooms*

differences between formal and informal high achievers, and between formal and informal low achievers, are both significant, and, as tables 4 to 6 in appendix D make clear, the major reason for this is the high incidence of play and chat in informal classrooms.

Teacher interaction (Figure 6.5 and table 7 in appendix D)

The incidence of teacher interaction is not very frequent in either type of classroom, but is higher in formal classrooms irrespective of achievement level. The only significant difference is

*When pupils were observed discussing work two tallies were recorded – a count was made both of work related interaction and of actual work, in order not to penalise informal classrooms.

among the high achievers, those in formal classrooms having significantly more interactions with teacher than those in informal classrooms. Again this finding is not easily interpreted

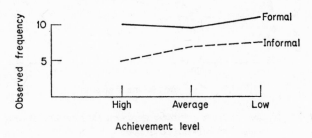

Figure 6.5 *Median scores for teacher interaction for three achievement levels in formal and informal classrooms*

because no distinction could be made in the schedule between an attempted response by a pupil, as when he puts his hand up for example, and an actual verbal response. This may have confounded this result.

Watching teacher (Table 8 in appendix D)
Since formal teachers tend to talk to the whole class more it follows that pupils in formal classes watch the teacher most. This is the case irrespective of achievement level, but reached significance only among the low achievers. This result is a little difficult to interpret, however, because there was no category for teacher talk in the schedule. It was not therefore possible to differentiate the pupil who watched the teacher during a period of teacher talk from one who cast wary glances around the classroom in order to ascertain the teacher's whereabouts. The category 'watching pupils' provided no significant differences across types of class or achievement levels (table 9 in appendix D).

Classroom movement (Figure 6.6 and table 10 in appendix D)
The findings on classroom movement are as might be expected. Informal pupils move around the class more, irrespective of achievement level. The trend is almost linear, a greater degree

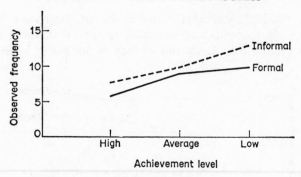

Figure 6.6 *Median scores for classroom movement for three achievement levels in formal and informal classrooms*

of movement being associated with lower achievers in both types of classroom.

Higher frequencies of movement are clearly associated with lower frequencies of fidgeting. Fidgeting is significantly more prevalent in formal classrooms, and in both increased fidgeting is associated with decreased achievement (figure 6.7 and table 11 in appendix D).

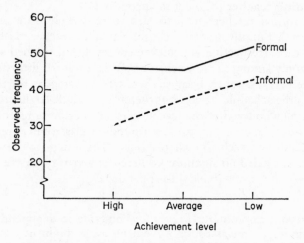

Figure 6.7 *Median scores for fidgeting for three achievement levels in formal and informal classrooms*

SUMMARY

The observational evidence clearly reveals that pupils in formal classrooms more frequently engage in work activity whatever their initial level of achievement. This is particularly marked in the areas of computation, writing, reading, and to a lesser extent making. The emphasis in such classrooms on the acquisition of basic skills is evident and could go some way to explaining the greater cognitive gain apparent under formal teaching styles.

In chapter 5 comment was made on the depressed performance of high achievers in informal classes. The observational evidence also provides clues as to why this might be. These pupils display a very low level of actual work activity, preferring to talk about it or simply gossip socially.

Very few differences emerged among average achievers, but this is not true for low achievers, a major feature being the large discrepancy between work activity among such children in formal and informal schools. It would seem that in a classroom where teacher direction is reduced the work involvement of high and low achieving pupils diminishes. At one end of the achievement continuum this could indicate that the bright child falls well behind his potential, whilst at the other end the less bright fails to gain the attention he needs.

Lack of work activity is made up by pupils in informal schools by increased frequencies of work related and social interaction. It could be argued that work related interaction is of benefit academically, but there is no evidence from this study to support this.

A clear link appears to emerge between work activity on the one hand and progress on the other. Formal pupils engage in more work activity and progress more than informal pupils, and high achieving informal pupils engage in little work related activity and substantially under-achieve.

In order to provide more evidence on this link, high and low achievers at post-test in each attainment area were contrasted on the observational evidence. The findings, which apply right across the formal/informal dimension, are considered briefly below.

High versus low achievers in reading
High achievers engaged in 21 per cent more work activity over-all. They did twice as much reading, twice as much computation, but slightly less writing. They have slightly less interaction with fellow pupils, be it work related or social. They move around the class less.

High versus low achievers in mathematics
High achievers engage in 23 per cent more actual work activity. They do substantially more computation and making things, and twice as much reading. They interact less with peers. They are less argumentative, exhibit less avoidance activity, move around the classroom less but interact with the teacher slightly more.

High versus low achievers in English
High achievers engage in 17 per cent more actual work activity, twice as much reading, substantially more computation and more making. Surprisingly they write less. They indulge in less peer interaction, noticeably in cooperative activities.

The finding that high English achievers write less is perhaps not as surprising as it at first seems. The writing category in the schedule includes all manner of writing, and writing *per se* does not guarantee good punctuation or comprehension. The link is thus not as direct as in the reading and computation categories.

The pattern clearly shows that high achievers work harder and interact less. However, the similarity of the three areas is in part due to the fact that many of the same pupils will be in each high or low category, artificially creating homogeneity. Nevertheless the analysis is one extra link in the chain linking work activity to pupil progress.

This chapter was written with the collaboration of Barbara Wade

7
Analyses of children's writing

IMAGINATIVE AND DESCRIPTIVE STORY WRITING

In a growing number of junior schools there is free, fluent and copious writing on a great variety of subject matter . . . Sometimes it is called 'creative writing', a rather grand name for it. Its essence is that much of it is personal and that the writers are communicating something that has really engaged their minds and their imaginations. To this kind of writing, here as in infant school, we give an unqualified welcome.

Despite this wholehearted approval by Plowden, the empirical and philosophical foundations of creative or imaginative writing are obscure. Shayer (1972) contends that the seminal work in fostering the notion in schools was the book *The Education of the Poetic Spirit* by Marjorie Hourd (1949). She defined the notion in terms of an amalgam of insights of a speculative nature drawn from the works of such psychologists as Spearman, Isaacs, Piaget, Koffka and Kohler, and the fundamental importance of imaginative perception in artistic creation as stressed in the works of Coleridge and Ruskin. In Hourd's view imagination has a central place in the educational process: it is through the active engagement of the child's imaginative powers that he is able to give meaning and shape to his emotional needs and to develop divergent habits of thinking. In judging such performances Hourd claimed that 'imaginative engagement' should be more highly valued than technical aspects of writing such as spelling, punctuation and grammar. What this meant in terms of teaching method was spelled out in a spate of books written from about 1950 onwards – books written by academics which discussed the philosophy and rationale of creative writing (Holbrook 1961; Creber 1966; Whitehead 1966) and books by practising teachers which specified methods, progressions and materials for use in the classroom (Langdon 1961; Walsh 1965; Rowe 1967).

Commitment to the value of creative writing would thus appear to spring from the belief that its production involves the child in an imaginative experience. By struggling to link a vivid experience to the appropriate language in which to express it, or, more fundamentally, to explore that area of his being in which experience and language intermingle, the child is held to have undergone a valuable developmental experience. His emotional growth has been fostered.

Such claims have not been subject to verification. Nevertheless, they have become part of the progressive teacher's value system and are supported by reference to experiences with children in the classroom and to published anecdotal material.

Sybil Marshall (1966), for example, has written accounts of her work which have been widely acclaimed by the proponents of creative writing. However, more recent writing on this topic appears to indicate a more healthy scepticism about the value of this emphasis where it is made at the expense of other kinds of writing. The following abstract from a group of teachers is included in the Bullock Report:

Many teachers see 'creative writing' as the high point of literacy. We need to re-think this: over-emphasis on it has distorted a whole view of language. It usually means, in actuality, colourful or fanciful language, not 'ordinary', using 'vivid imagery'. It is often false, artificially stimulated and pumped up by the teacher or written to an unconscious model which he has given to the children. It is very often divorced from real feeling.

The report argues that the term has come to mean many things and that lack of an agreed definition reflects the absence of a clear rationale for the work to which it refers, and this applies equally to such terms as 'free', 'expression' and 'personal'.

Since the development of creative writing is highly valued by informal teachers, and since the literature reviewed in chapter 2 indicates that creativity may be enhanced by more informal methods, the range of attainment criteria was widened to include an imaginative story and a descriptive story. The former was designed to evaluate the pupils' use of ideas and imagination, unencumbered by constraints of spelling, punctuation and grammar, whilst the latter was to assess the pupils' powers of accurate description, taking grammar and spelling into account.

Previous research into the assessment of imaginative story writing (Bennett 1972 and 1973b) provided useful guidelines for the present study. In pilot experiments it was demonstrated that (a) impression marking by practising primary school teachers was as reliable as a prearranged marking scheme, and that the correlation between the two methods of marking was very high; (b) a single stimulus was preferable to a choice of topic since certain topics were more amenable to originality; and (c) that a topic based on 'invisibility' was appropriate for top junior classes and appealed equally to both boys and girls.

In the light of this earlier experience the pupils were introduced to the topic by being provided with an introductory paragraph which put them into a situation whereby they were invisible for a day. They were then invited to complete the story. To overcome any problems with poor readers the teacher also read out the introductory passage and informed the pupils that good ideas and imagination were required and that poor spelling and grammar would not be penalised.

It was felt that the descriptive story should be clearly grounded in the child's immediate experience and it was thus decided to ask the pupils to write an essay entitled 'What I did at school yesterday'. After informing the pupils of the topic the teacher then instructed them to be as accurate as possible, and that in this instance spelling and grammar would be taken into consideration. A content analysis of this essay provided evidence of the validity of the teaching styles outlined in chapter 3.

In the previous study it was ascertained that most pupils had completed their stories in twenty minutes. It was felt that for the imaginative story in particular a stringent time limit should not be set. The teachers were therefore told that most pupils should have finished within half an hour, but asked to allow extra time should pupils require it.

Although there is no empirical evidence on variation in standards of marking by different types of teacher it was envisaged that differences in standards might occur. In order to circumvent this, each essay was marked by three teachers, one formal, one mixed, and one informal. This arrangement served a dual purpose, firstly to increase the reliability of marks, and secondly to ascertain whether in fact there is a discernible difference in marking standards. All thirty-seven teachers were involved in the marking, although they did not know from which school(s) the scripts had come. All grading was on a fifteen point scale.

Results

Table 1 in appendix E presents the inter-marker correlations for both stories. The relationships are slightly more homogeneous for the imaginative story, ranging from 0·62 to 0·65, whereas those for the descriptive writing range between 0·56 to 0·66. The median correlation of 0·86 is somewhat higher than many reported studies on the reliability of essay marking, which indicates a high degree of agreement between markers.

Whether teachers of different styles marked to different standards can be ascertained from table 7.1. No clear divergence is

| Teaching style of marker | Imaginative | | | | | | Descriptive | | | | | |
| | Boys | | | Girls | | | Boys | | | Girls | | |
	I	M	F	I	M	F	I	M	F	I	M	F
Informal	7·7	6.5	7·4	8·3	8·3	8.5	7.8	6·6	7·5	8.9	8·3	8·5
Mixed	7·2	6·8	7·9	8·1	8·0	8·6	7·8	7·0	7·5	8·9	8·2	8·6
Formal	6·6	6·7	7·4	8·0	8·1	8·4	7·1	6·8	7·4	8·1	8·1	8·8
Total average mark	7·2	6·7	7·6	8·1	8·1	8·5	7·6	6·8	7·5	8·6	8·2	8·6

Table 7.1 *Imaginative and descriptive story marks by sex, teaching style, and teaching style of marker*

discernible between informal and mixed teachers, but formal teachers do appear to be using more rigorous standards. This is most noticeable in their marking of essays from informal schools, which are consistently given a lower mark than when marked by informal and mixed teachers.

Also included in the table are the average essay marks of boys and girls by style of teaching. These are plotted graphically in figure 7.1.

Figure 7.1 *Scores for imaginative and descriptive story writing by sex and teaching style*

Two clear patterns emerge from the data, a sex difference and a teaching style difference. The strongest effect is the sex difference: girls are shown to score more highly than boys irrespective of teaching style. This is a common finding at this age level.

The pattern of scores across teaching styles is very similar for both types of story, showing that formal and informal pupils perform equally well, whereas pupils in mixed classes perform at a slightly lower level.

The differences are quite small and indicate no clear superiority of any one teaching style. There is little in these results to support the widely held view that informal teaching produces pupils who are more likely to respond more imaginatively in writing than do those who are being taught more formally. On the other hand there is no evidence from this study to support the opposing argument that informal pupils fall behind their formal counterparts in written work as far as grammatical accuracy is concerned. This latter argument is somewhat weaker since it is based on the assumption that the markers have taken this aspect into consideration in their impression marking. This is difficult to establish. A correlation of 0·77 was found between the marks for the two stories, which indicates that those who scored highly on one story tended to score highly on the other, and vice versa. At least two possible interpretations of this finding are possible – that common abilities are required for both types of writing, or that teachers used the same implicit criteria in their impression marking of both sets of stories. To assess which interpretation is correct would require another study.

It could be argued that teachers should have attended a briefing session before the marking to agree on criteria and standards, but this would have vitiated the whole objective of the study, namely, to gain evaluations of written work from class teachers based on the standards and criteria they normally adopt in ongoing classroom assessment. Nevertheless, criteria for marking different types of pupil writing might be a fruitful topic for inservice courses.

PUNCTUATION AND SPELLING

The view is growing that informal teaching pays scant attention to English grammar and leaves children ill-equipped for secondary school. Since it was not possible to test the validity of this view from the impression marking, a second study was undertaken in which punctuation and spelling errors were investigated in detail.

There is little previous research in this area except by 'O' and 'A' level examiners. Many educationalists appear to regard an assessment of pupils' work for mechanical accuracy as a distortion of the purposes of writing, arguing perhaps with some justification that an over-emphasis on mechanical accuracy destroys creativity and the self-confidence of pupils. One of the few studies that relates to the assessment of children's writing was the Schools Council project 'The development of writing abilities'. However, the categories in the system developed by Britton (1971) are not descriptive of how language is used, but of how the writer adapts his language to suit the examiner or the audience for which he writes, in order to communicate effectively in different circumstances. The system is not concerned with standards of correctness, but rather with developing the teacher's awareness of the different purposes for which language is used by children in written work, and with providing criteria for analysing children's writing according to the function it is intended to perform.

However, Britton was instrumental in devising the only marking scheme for mechanical accuracy which was found in a review of the literature. This was devised as an experimental marking scheme for the new 'O' level English Language paper of the Cambridge Examination Board (Britton, Martin and Rosen 1966). Unfortunately this scheme was not found to be suitable for this study, and a new system was developed, the categories of which were built up from the errors found in the stories themselves. It was devised by Statham (1976) to provide, in the language of the Bullock Report, 'a simple measure of correctness in grammar, usage, punctuation and spelling'; in other words a measure of technical competence.

The category instrument was developed by taking random samples of scripts from each of the three general teaching styles and marking them in detail. The categories emanating from this process were then expanded and modified by marking further random samples of stories. In this way the categories were developed from the errors in the stories themselves rather than being based on some arbitrary, externally imposed standards of accuracy in writing. The final version of the instrument known as MAM (Mechanical Accuracy Measure) contains four categories: punctuation, phonetic misspellings. misspellings by analogy, and carelessness, the sub-categories of which are detailed below.

Category 1 – Punctuation (P)

1.1	PC	Capital letter omitted, or haphazard use of capitals
1.2	PF	Omission of full stop, or haphazard use of full stop
1.3	PFa	Omission of full stop in abbreviations (e.g. PE or Mr)
1.4	PA	Apostrophe in abbreviations omitted or in the wrong place (e.g. hadnt; had'nt)
1.5	PG	Apostrophe omitted or in the wrong place in genitives (e.g. teachers desk; five boy's books)
1.6	PGA	Confusion of genitives with plurals – redundant apostrophe by analogy with genitives (e.g. The boys' went to the baths' with two teachers'.)
1.7	PK	No comma used to separate items in a list, or words in apposition to a noun from the noun, or, in direct speech, to separate words in inverted

commas from the words which introduce them; misuse of comma

1.8 PQ   Misuse or omission of quotation marks

1.9 PO   Other misuse of punctuation marks (dash; brackets; etc.)

Category 2 – Phonetic misspellings (PH)

2.1 PH   Phonetic misspellings (e.g. 'chiken', 'peaple', 'enverlopes', 'com', 'whissle', 'pudden', 'dinar')

2.2 PHC   Word-pairs confused – same part of speech (e.g. 'beach' for 'beech'; 'sinking' for 'singing'), or high frequency words confused (e.g. 'a' for 'an'/ 'and'; 'in' for 'into'; 'from' for 'to')

2.3 PHG   Word-pairs confused – different parts of speech (e.g. 'I rote' for 'I wrote'; 'right' for 'write'; 'are' for 'our'; 'off' for 'of'; 'man' for 'men' (irregular plural))

2.4 PHU   Gross misspelling; word unidentifiable; more than three letters wrong (e.g. 'precats' for 'croquettes'; 'halardy' for 'heraldry'; 'uphirraytos' for 'apparatus'; 'asmbe' for 'assembly'; 'pottoes' for 'photograph')

2.5 PHA   Faulty word-attack – letters in the wrong sequence (e.g. 'ot' for 'to'; 'paly' for 'play'; 'hared' for 'heard'; 'gorups' for 'groups'; 'coulers' for 'colours')

Category 3 – Analogy (misspellings by analogy) (A)

3.1 AR   In word-building: root retained intact when one letter should be modified (e.g. 'dayly' for 'daily'), or final consonant of a monosyllable not doubled (e.g. 'wraped' for 'wrapped'; 'drumer' for 'drummer'), or two parts of a word not joined to form one word (e.g. 'in side' for 'inside'; 'in to' for 'into'), or wrong root built upon (e.g. 'rehearsaled' for 'rehearsed')

3.2 AE   In word-building: extra letters (e.g. 'untill' for 'until'; 'comeing' for 'coming'), words not 'telescoped' or spelt by analogy to similar sounding words (e.g. 'hopping' for 'hoping' – possible confusion after dropping mute 'e' and before adding '-ing')

3.3 AI   Inversion – spelling rule ' "i" before "e" except after "c" ' misunderstood and misapplied (e.g. 'recieve' for 'receive'; 'iether' for 'either')

3.4 AT   Words wrongly 'telescoped' (e.g. 'altogether' for 'all together' – instructions in a singing lesson) or two words joined together when they should not be (e.g. 'dinnermoney' for 'dinner money')

Category 4 – Carelessness (C)

4.1 C   Carelessness – an obvious slip (e.g. initial 'p' for 'b' in scripts where there are no other problems with letter orientation)

4.2 CI   Carelessness – inconsistent spelling of a word, including the correct spelling

4.3 I   Word used several times in a variety of forms which does not include the correct one

4.4 MW   Word left out ('we done'; 'half-hour' for 'half an hour')

4.5 CG   In nouns: '-s' left out of plural form
In verbs: '-s' omitted from third person singular, present tense; '-d'/'-ed' omitted from past tense
False concord (e.g. 'we was')
Redundant relative pronoun or misuse of relative pronoun

4.6 CO   Orientation: 'd' for 'b'; 'p' for 'b'; 'b' for 'p' (e.g. 'rudder' for 'rubber'; 'dack' for 'back'; 'put' for 'but'; 'but' for 'put')

Analysis

For the purpose of analysis a matched sample of forty-eight boys and forty-eight girls was drawn from each teaching style, resulting in 288 descriptive stories. They were matched from their results on the English test since this involved aspects of grammar and comprehension.

The length of stories varied between 100 and 500 words, and in order to avoid distortion Britton's example of marking the first 200 words was adopted. Where stories were shorter than this, proportional adjustments were made. Stories were marked in random order to obviate any possibility of a marking 'set'.

Punctuation

65 per cent of all errors appeared in this category. Figure 7.2 (and table 2 in appendix E) shows the scores for boys and girls in each teaching style.

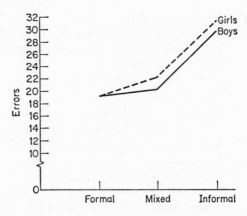

Figure 7.2 *Punctuation errors by sex and teaching style*

Although girls tend to make slightly more errors than boys, the largest differences relate to teaching style. Pupils from informal classes make significantly more punctuation errors than those in mixed or formal classes. The areas where the discrepancies are most noticeable are omission or haphazard use of capital letters and full stops, misuse of the comma and misuse or omission of quotation marks.

Phonetic misspelling

35 per cent of all errors were spelling mistakes, and of this proportion 25 per cent occurred in the phonetic category. A different error pattern is evident here, as can be seen in figure 7.3 (and table 3 in appendix E), sex differences being more prominent

than teaching style discrepancies. Girls make fewer errors of this kind, the group with fewest errors being girls in informal classrooms, whereas boys in informal classrooms make the most.

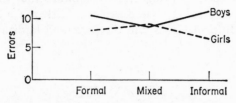

Figure 7.3 *Phonetic misspellings by sex and teaching style*

Misspellings by analogy

Misspellings by analogy are fairly infrequent, this category containing only 3 per cent of total errors. They are less likely to be made by girls, and more likely to occur in informal classrooms (figure 7.4 and table 4 in appendix E).

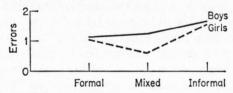

Figure 7.4 *Misspelling by analogy by sex and teaching style*

Carelessness

Mistakes due to carelessness represent 7 per cent of total errors. Pupils in formal classes make fewest errors of this kind and those in mixed classes the most (figure 7.5 and table 5 in appendix E).

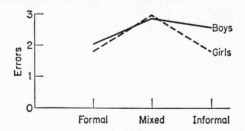

Figure 7.5 *Carelessness by sex and teaching style*

The sub-categories where the greatest discrepancy is found are the omission of apostrophes, false concord, and misuse of the relative pronoun.

When the spelling categories are summed they indicate a sex rather than a teaching style difference. Girls make fewer errors than boys. Informal girls win the prize and informal boys take the booby.

SUMMARY

Two separate studies were undertaken to investigate different yet related aspects of pupil writing. The impression marking carried out by teachers revealed few differences that could be attributed to teaching style, which provides no support for the notion that informal teaching engenders higher quality output in this area. On the other hand the view that informal teaching can depress performance in grammar is only partially upheld. Formal and mixed pupils showed a clear superiority in punctuation but spelling errors appear to be more related to sex than classroom practice. However, the fact that formal pupils are better at punctuation and no worse in spelling and imaginative story marks would seem to indicate that it is possible to achieve grammatical accuracy without detriment to creative output. The myth that this cannot be so is fairly prevalent.

A final word should be said about the inferential quality of the data. These data are weaker in this respect than the data relating to progress contained in chapter 5. It was not possible to analyse change in story writing performance and as a result it is less easy to tie the results to differences in teaching style. It would be safer therefore to attribute the differences noted to a school rather than a teaching effect.

8

Pupil personality and academic progress

Teachers have long felt that the personality of pupils is an important variable in the classroom. In one of the few British studies which have assessed teacher reactions to the personality and behaviour of pupils Morrison and McIntyre (1969) found that the reactions tended to fall into three major groups: pupil attainment; general classroom behaviour and attitudes towards the teacher; and cheerfulness, social confidence and cooperation with peers. They asked a sample of primary school teachers to create an order of merit of pupil attributes that were of most concern to them. The nine attributes of highest concern were: general ability, carelessness, laziness, talkativeness, cooperativeness, persistence, courtesy, ability to use language and originality.

These characteristics are of importance to teachers, but are they of importance to academic attainment? Investigations into this link proliferated during the 1960s but no clear picture emerged, as Entwistle (1972) showed in his review of that period. He argued that it was dangerous to assume wide generality in statements about these relationships, since many factors, including age, sex, geographical area, teaching method and teacher personality, may all affect the relationship to some extent. He concluded 'It still requires considerable faith and imagination to see where these results may lead.'

The approach used in research into pupil personality has attracted considerable criticism, relating to the bankruptcy of the theoretical rationale, the poor construction and unknown validity of the inventories used, and the mode of statistical analysis adopted.

A thesis which now appears to be generally accepted is that classroom behaviour results from the interaction of the classroom environment, with its pattern of demands and expectations, and the personality of the pupils (Getzels and Thelen 1960; Mischel 1968; Argyle and Little 1972; Sells 1973). Thus the basic behavioural dimensions in any classroom situation will depend upon the relative strengths of both sets of influences, and, as has been argued previously (Bennett and Youngman 1973), it could be that in the school setting institutional demands may be sufficiently strong to swamp the effects of individual differences in personality. However, this thesis is as yet unexamined because personality inventories currently available tend to contain items of a general nature which fail to take differences in social situation into account. In a small scale but interesting study by Best (1973) it was found that even when pupils completed the Junior Eysenck Personality Inventory in the classroom they answered 80 per cent of the items with reference to their feelings and behaviour at home. Correlating responses on such inventories with school attainment is thus answering the question 'What is the relationship between pupils' perception of their feelings and behaviour at home to their attainment at school?' It seems clear that in addition to remedying the known defects in the questionnaires commonly used (Peterson 1965; Howarth and Browne 1971, 1972; Bennett 1973a), inventories need to be designed which have a clear meaning for particular social situations.

Pupil type has been narrowly defined in previous studies because of the reliance on correlation methods in relating individual traits such as extroversion or anxiety to attainment. Entwistle (1972) alluded to this problem and suggested the creation of types by cluster analysis – by grouping pupils together on the basis of a larger range of personality attributes. A preliminary analysis along these lines was undertaken by Bennett and Youngman who proposed a model of personality and behaviour in school based on the two dimensions of adjustment–maladjustment and assertion–compliance. However, this did not resolve the question of how many personality characteristics are necessary to create valid types. Sells (1963) estimated that more than one hundred different attributes would have to be accommodated if a full and sufficient explanation of human behaviour were to be achieved. His conclusion was that the behavioural scientists will have to be satisfied with either partial explanations or conditional explanations as an interim alternative to perfection. In relating this to the classroom researcher Adams (1970b) stressed the law of parsimony in delineating as key variables those which both have the greatest predictive and explanatory power and can be used with a minimum of effort.

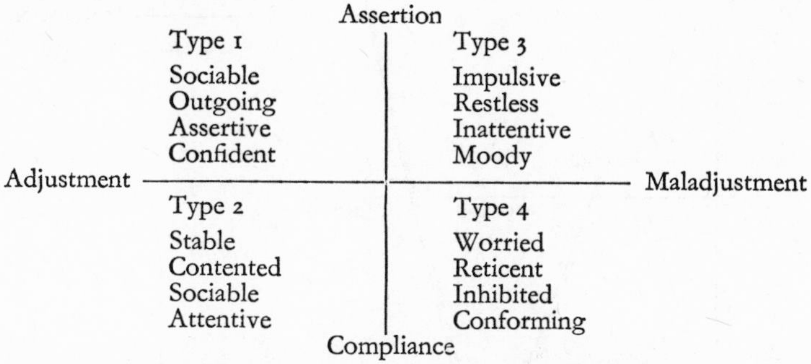

Assertion

	Type 1	Type 3	
	Sociable	Impulsive	
	Outgoing	Restless	
	Assertive	Inattentive	
	Confident	Moody	
Adjustment			Maladjustment
	Type 2	Type 4	
	Stable	Worried	
	Contented	Reticent	
	Sociable	Inhibited	
	Attentive	Conforming	

Compliance

Figure 8.1 *Two dimensions underlying four personality types*

These lines of reasoning underlie the methodology and measurement adopted in this study. A wide range of personality attributes were initially chosen, including those which had provided most predictive power in earlier research, but these were supplemented by behavioural dimensions not previously included in personality inventories. In all but the self concept questionnaire all items were worded to relate to the school and classroom situation. The self concept was measured by a semantic differential technique, the constructs of which were derived from essays written by pupils in formal and informal schools. Full details of the theoretical rationale and scale development can be found in Jordan (1976), Long (1976) and Wade (1976).

The traits measured, together with the mean scores at pre- and post-test, short- and long-term reliability estimates and internal stability co-efficients are provided in table 1 in appendix F.

Overall little change occurs in mean scores from pre- to post-test, although there is some indication of a slight deterioration in behaviour, since the mean score for contentiousness and unsociability increases, whilst those for conformity, attitude to school and motivation decrease. On the other hand, the levels of anxiety and neuroticism also diminish.

Analyses were undertaken to establish whether the extent of

change from pre- to post-test was related to teaching style. In the main these analyses showed that teaching approaches had little effect. The two exceptions were motivation and anxiety which exhibited the interesting parallel pattern seen in figure 8.2.

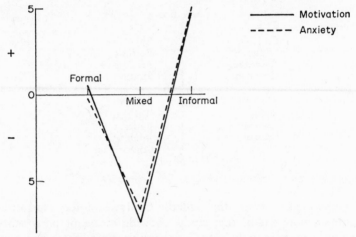

Figure 8.2 *Change in motivation and anxiety by teaching style*

Change is minimal among formal pupils, but motivation and anxiety decrease among mixed pupils and increase in informal classrooms. There is thus some justification here for the argument that informal teaching engenders more favourable attitudes to school and schoolwork, although the parallel finding for anxiety might not have been expected. It is a finding which was apparent in our earlier work in this area, and one that can be interpreted in many ways. Perhaps the explanation which carries most theoretical validity is that many pupils, particularly the anxious and insecure, find that unstructured teaching and classroom environments increase their anxiety. Further evidence on this aspect will be presented later in the chapter.

SELF CONCEPT

There was no evidence of differential change of self concept or esteem across teaching styles. However, additional analyses were carried out in this area since it can be argued from social psychological theories that teaching styles could make a difference in the way the pupils perceive their role, because of the manner in which pupil interaction is encouraged or discouraged. It could be argued that formal classroom organisations generate conformity to socially defined and expected pupil roles whereas informal organisations may encourage individual expression of the self. If so, this should be reflected in the perceptions of the pupils about themselves and each other, with greater differentiation being apparent in informal classrooms and more stereotyped concepts of self and others in formal classrooms.

Two instruments were developed to assess these aspects, the semantic differential already referred to, and a measure based on sociometric technique similar to that used by Minuchin and others (1969). In this pupils were asked to nominate those pupils in their class who were most like and least like a list of behavioural stereotypes provided, e.g. 'the children that I most often work with', 'Here is a child who usually does as he is told and is good at his work.'

These analyses of the stereotype data, which were restricted to the formal and informal classrooms, revealed a strong underlying trend for pupils to rate each other on a good–bad dimension in both types of classroom. In other words, there was no evidence to suggest that pupils perceived each other differently in formal and informal classes, which offers no support for the theory. In both classroom types boys were rated less favourably than girls, but this trend was more apparent in formal situations.

Sociograms based on pupil popularity ratings were also drawn. A number of these indicated that perhaps a more complex, integrated social structure existed in informal classrooms. One interpretation of such evidence, which is considered fully in Jordan (1976), is that the type of social structure created in informal classrooms derives from the greater degree of pupil movement and interaction.

There was no difference in level of self esteem in formal and informal classrooms.

Summary

It had been hypothesised that teaching style would have an effect upon the way that the pupils perceive themselves and others.

This was not found to be the case, the main feature of the analyses being the finding of insignificant differences between types of classroom. There is some indication that the development of a more complex and focused social structure may be engendered by informal styles of teaching, perhaps because of increased pupil movement and interaction. No differences in level of self esteem were found between formal and informal pupils and no significant change in level occurred over the school year.

PUPIL PERSONALITY AND ACADEMIC PROGRESS

Most studies on the relationship between pupil personality and attainment have suffered from a common weakness – the almost exclusive reliance on correlational techniques, which lead to the problem of definition of pupil types, as Entwistle (1972) has pointed out. In addition, correlational techniques compare similarity between *tests* whereas it is obviously more valid to consider differences between *pupils*. For this reason a typology of pupils was computed which grouped pupils together on the basis of the similarity of their personality profiles. The statistical process was the same as that used in calculating the typology of teaching styles. Statistical criteria indicated that eight pupil groupings represented the optimal solution and these are described below.

Type 1
This comprises a group of 150 pupils, 85 boys and 65 girls. They are fairly average in most respects although they profess to be somewhat stable and extroverted with a reasonable conception of their own ability. They are also more motivated than average, which indicates a positive attitude to school and schoolwork.

Type 2
There are 103 pupils in this group, 39 boys and 64 girls. They are very introverted and neurotic with a high degree of classroom anxiety. They hold a poor view of their own ability and tend to be both unsociable and non-conforming.

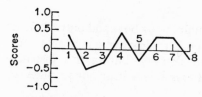

Figure 8.3 *Type 1*

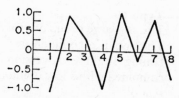

Figure 8.4 *Type 2*

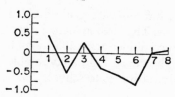

Figure 8.5 *Type 3*

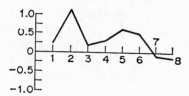

Figure 8.6 *Type 4*

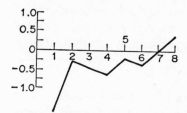

Figure 8.7 *Type 5*

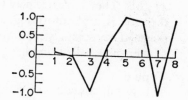

Figure 8.8 *Type 6*

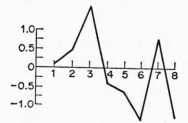

Figure 8.9 *Type 7*

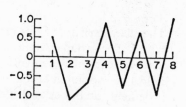

Figure 8.10 *Type 8*

Key

1 Extroversion	2 Neuroticism
3 Contentiousness	4 Self evaluation
5 Anxiety	6 Motivation
7 Associability	8 Conformity

Type 3
This is a large group of 150, containing 92 boys and only 58 girls. They hold in common with type 1 a fairly average profile containing slight extroversion and stability, but in this instance combined with a low opinion of themselves and poor attitudes to school.

Type 4
This is another large group of 150, but almost equally divided between the sexes: 73 boys and 77 girls. The most evident characteristic is a high level of neuroticism combined with a fairly high level of classroom anxiety. They do, however, hold a favourable impression of themselves, and positive attitudes to school.

Type 5
This is the smallest group, containing only 78 pupils, 31 boys and 47 girls. They are extremely introverted, hold a poor opinion of themselves, are conforming, and have a slight tendency to neuroticism. They strongly resemble a type found in previous research which was labelled timid.

Type 6
This group contains 108 pupils, but is composed almost entirely of girls: 91 girls as against only 17 boys. These pupils show a high level of classroom anxiety but they hold a very positive attitude to school, are non-contentious, sociable and conforming.

Type 7
The characteristics of this group are in stark contrast to those of type 6. The group contains 98 pupils, only 22 of whom are girls. They are extremely contentious, non-conforming, unsociable and hold a poor opinion of school and schoolwork. They tend to be a little neurotic but show little anxiety in the classroom context.

Type 8
If type 7 could be labelled sinners, then this group could be labelled saints. 113 pupils comprise this type, 58 boys and 52 girls. They are stable, extroverted, motivated, sociable, conforming and hold a favourable self image – a teacher's dream.

Computation of residual gain scores for each type allows an assessment of the effect of pupil type on academic progress.

Differential gain by pupil type

Reading
None of the overall differences are large but the trends are as might have been expected from previous research at this age level.

Type	Overall	Boys	Girls
1	0·6	0·7	0·6
2	−1·8	−2·5	−1·4
3	0·6	0·5	0·8
4	0	0·4	−0·4
5	−1·0	−2·5	1·5
6	0	4·7	−0·8
7	−0·3	−0·2	−0·6
8	0·3	0·9	−0·4

Table 8.1 *Differential gain by pupil types in reading*

The two groups with the highest gain are both characterised by stability and extroversion, and the group with least gain hold the opposite attributes, neuroticism and introversion.

The sex differences are slight except in types 5 (timid) and 6 (anxious conformists). Both of these are dominated by females but the effect is opposite in each case. Timid boys progress considerably less well than the girls whereas anxious conformist boys progress considerably better.

Mathematics
Least progress is again associated with children of introverted and neurotic characteristics, but overall the differences are slight.

Type	Overall	Boys	Girls
1	−0·4	−0·2	−0·6
2	−1·7	−1·4	−1·9
3	−0·3	−0·6	0·2
4	0·6	−0·2	1·2
5	−1·1	−0·5	−1·4
6	0·8	3·0	0·4
7	0·7	0·6	1·2
8	0·3	0·6	0

Table 8.2 *Differential gain by pupil types in mathematics*

It is interesting to note that the greatest sex difference occurs once again among the anxious conformists (type 6), where the boys in an essentially feminine group progress considerably better than the girls.

English
Another series of small differences, the sinners (type 7) progressing least and the saints (type 8) the most. The same sex difference again occurs in type 6 (anxious conformists) and to a smaller extent in the opposite direction in type 2 (unmotivated extroverts), whose boys gain considerably less than their female counterparts.

Type	Overall	Boys	Girls
1	0·8	−0·1	2·1
2	−0·9	−2·3	−0·1
3	−0·1	0·5	−0·8
4	−0·3	−0·1	−0·6
5	−0·6	−1·6	0·1
6	0·7	3·2	0·2
7	−1·0	−0·9	−1·2
8	1·1	1·2	1·0

Table 8.3 *Differential gain by pupil type in English*

Overall there appear to be few differences in the progress of children with different personality characteristics. This result may have occurred because pupils of the same personality type perform differently in classrooms of differing teaching style. Analyses were therefore carried out relating gain, pupil type and teaching style.

Differential gain by pupil type and teaching style

Reading
It will be recalled that mixed styles tend to be associated with most progress in reading and informal styles with least progress. This trend is clearly seen in table 8.4.

With the exception of type 2 pupils all personality types in mixed classes perform better than expected. Gains outweigh losses in formal styles, with types 1 (motivated stable extroverts) and 8 (saints) showing greatest gains and sinners (type 7) least.

With informal styles all but type 6 pupils (anxious conformists) progress less well, often substantially less well, than expected. A look across teaching styles reveals some large discrepancies in gain of pupils of the same personality type who happen to be

Type	Formal	Mixed	Informal
1	1·7	0·5	−0·2
2	0	−2·8	−2·2
3	1·1	2·6	−2·5
4	0·3	3·2	−3·6
5	−0·7	1·2	−0·5
6	−0·2	0·9	0
7	−1·5	1·5	−1·0
8	1·7	1·1	−1·7

Table 8.4 *Differential gain by pupil type and teaching style in reading*

taught by different styles. The greatest differences occur in types 2, 3, 4 and 8. Type 2 are anxious introverts and such pupils perform much better in formal classrooms, which supports previous research on this topic.

Type 3 and 4 pupils appear to thrive most under mixed styles, both under-achieving badly in informal classes. Type 4 pupils are also characterised by their high degree of neuroticism, which adds further weight to the argument relating neuroticism/anxiety to classroom structure. Among the saints (type 8) the relationship with teaching style is linear, best in formal and worst in informal.

Mathematics
A stronger effect of teaching style is apparent here with all pupils, irrespective of personality types, gain being associated with

Type	Formal	Mixed	Informal
1	2·0	−2·7	0
2	0·2	−3·5	−1·3
3	3·0	−1·3	−1·8
4	1·7	−0·4	−0·4
5	0·6	−3·5	−0·7
6	3·6	−0·9	−1·6
7	0·7	−0·5	1·8
8	2·0	1·4	−2·1

Table 8.5 *Differential gain by pupil types and teaching style in mathematics*

formal styles and under-achievement with mixed and informal classes.

An examination of differences in the gains of pupil types across teaching styles indicates that large discrepancies exist. The anxious and introverted pupils again perform considerably better in formal classrooms, as do the saints (type 8). Perhaps of most interest, however, is the performance of the sinners (type 7), since in this instance greater progress is made in informal classrooms.

English

The picture here is similar to that in mathematics with all pupil types showing gains in formal classrooms, and most types in

Type	Formal	Mixed	Informal
1	4·1	−0·8	−0·6
2	0·3	−1·1	−1·7
3	1·0	−0·2	−0·5
4	1·0	−1·0	−1·9
5	0·9	−1·0	−1·5
6	1·2	1·9	−0·2
7	0·5	−0·2	−3·0
8	2·6	1·6	−0·8

Table 8.6 *Differential gain by pupil type and teaching style in English*

mixed and informal classrooms under-achieving. The performance of pupils of type 7 (sinners) is not consistent with the finding in mathematics, however, since in English they progress substantially less than expected in informal classrooms.

An attempt is made in figure 8.11 to summarise differential gain by pupil type and teaching style, by plotting the average gain in all three academic subjects for each type. From this it is quite clear that the answer to the question 'Do pupils of the same personality type show differential progress under different types of teaching?' is unequivocally in the affirmative. All but the sinners perform better, often substantially better, in formal classrooms. This is particularly noticeable among the groups which contain the most high achieving pupils – types 1 and 8. In both, progress is much greater under formal teaching than expected, and in the case of the saints is substantially below expectation in informal classrooms. It was shown in chapter 5 that the perform-

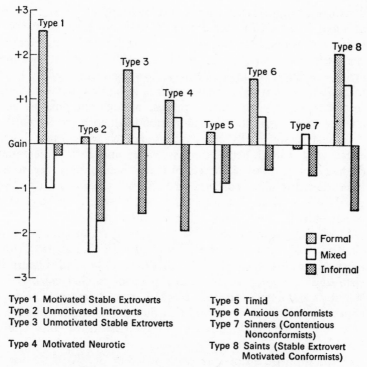

Type 1 Motivated Stable Extroverts
Type 2 Unmotivated Introverts
Type 3 Unmotivated Stable Extroverts
Type 4 Motivated Neurotic

Type 5 Timid
Type 6 Anxious Conformists
Type 7 Sinners (Contentious Nonconformists)
Type 8 Saints (Stable Extrovert Motivated Conformists)

Figure 8.11 *Differential progress by type of pupil and teaching style*

ance of initially high achieving pupils was facilitated under formal teaching, and these findings lend force to that argument. Large differences in progress are also apparent in types 3 and 4, the unmotivated stable extroverts and the motivated neurotics.

In general the effectiveness of mixed teaching is somewhere in between formal and informal, although it appears to be particularly ineffective for the unmotivated anxious introverts, but most effective for the sinners, though this latter effect is marginal.

SUMMARY

A large battery of personality tests was administered at pre- and post-test. Little change took place in the mean scores although there was some indication that attitudes and behaviour may have

deteriorated slightly over that period. The scores for contentiousness and unsociability increase whilst those for conformity, attitude to school and motivation decrease. In analysing differential
change in personality attributes under the three general teaching
styles, only motivation and anxiety showed a marked effect, both
increasing in informal classrooms. It is suggested that a possible
reason for this is that many pupils, notably the anxious and
insecure, find unstructured organisation antithetical to their needs.

In analyses of pupils' self concept and self esteem few differences were found between classrooms, and little differential
change took place over the school year. There is, however, some
indication that more complex and focused social structures are
developed in informal classrooms, possibly because of the greater
opportunity for pupil movement and interaction.

In relating types of pupils to progress in reading, maths and
English, few differences were found overall, though least progress was made by groups whose characteristics included neuroticism and introversion, and most by groups characterised by
stability and extroversion. Marked sex differences seldom
appeared, though it was found that the anxious conformist boys
of type 6, which is dominated by girls, performed consistently
better than the girls in that group.

A question of major interest is whether pupils of the same
personality type progress differentially under different teaching
styles. The answer is unequivocally in the affirmative. This was
particularly noticeable among the personality types containing
the high achievers, i.e. the motivated stable extroverts (type 1)
and the saints (type 8), who substantially over-achieved under
formal teaching and under-achieved under informal teaching.
This pattern was also true for types 3 and 4. Mixed teaching
appears to be particularly ineffective for type 2 children, though
marginally most effective for the sinners.

Overall the effect of teaching style is much more powerful than
the effect of personality type, most pupils showing more substantial progress in formal classrooms. It would therefore appear that
the demands of the teaching environment do tend to swamp the
effect of personality, an argument taken further in the next
chapter, which presents evidence on the classroom behaviour of
pupils of the same personality type under different teaching styles.

9

Pupil personality and classroom behaviour

The analyses presented in the previous chapter are still one step removed from reality. Researchers have very little conception of how responses to personality questionnaires relate to actual behaviour. In an attempt to throw some light on this problem the classroom behaviour of pupils in each of the eight types was examined and compared.

The observational data on the 101 pupils in formal and informal classes were used for this purpose. Since the pupil sample was necessarily chosen before the creation of the typology described in chapter 8, the number of pupils in each type varied between four in type 2 to twenty-one in type 6. It is therefore likely that all types are adequately represented. Statistical significance was ascertained by using Kruskal–Wallis analyses of variance and U tests, but given the nature of the sample it is safer to regard these analyses as exploratory.

In the analyses that follow, personality types are related to each of the behavioural categories in the observation schedule, formal and informal classrooms being treated separately.

Actual work

It was shown in chapter 6 that levels of actual work are lower in informal classrooms, and this is clearly seen in figure 9.1. In none of the personality types is work higher under informal teaching styles. In general terms the lowest frequency of work is exhibited by the anxious introvert of type 2 and the anxious pupils of type 4, although there is a large discrepancy between pupils of this latter type in formal and informal classrooms, which provides one more piece of evidence to suggest the unsuitability of informal classroom environments for anxious pupils.

Large differences also appear among other types of pupil. Both the sinners and the saints work considerably more in formal classrooms, as do the stable extroverts of type 1.

Work related pupil interaction

Work related pupil interaction is generally higher in informal classrooms, and this is visible in the fairly complex pattern shown in figure 9.2. In this category of behaviour it is interesting to note that the three pupil types characterised by anxiety – 2, 4 and 6 – show great similarity of behaviour in the two classroom contexts. On the other hand large discrepancies exist in three groups, 5, 7 and 8. The greatest divergence is seen in type 5 pupils, the timid, conforming introverts. These interact very little in formal classes but do so more than average in the informal situation. The opposite pattern is true of the sinners, who interact much less in the informal classroom context.

Pupil social interaction

Social interaction was found to be much more frequent in informal classrooms, and in figure 9.3 it can be seen that this is true of all personality types. In fact there are few differences between the classroom contexts here. The anxious types all talk the most, irrespective of teaching style, whereas the timid pupils and saints talk least, probably for similar reasons. Both these groups have a high frequency of actual work, a state of affairs which precludes a high level of interaction.

Teacher interaction

Overall the anxious introverts of type 2 interact with their teachers the most, the pattern being identical in both formal and informal classrooms. Large differences do occur in some personality types, however, notably types 4, 5 and 8. In each case there is a higher level of interaction in the formal situation. The largest discrepancy occurs amongst the saints, who, incidentally, are also a high achieving group. Saints in formal classes have a far greater frequency of contact with their teacher than their counterparts in informal classrooms.

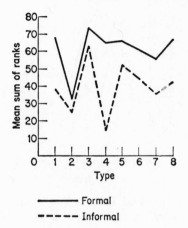

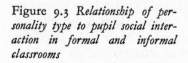

Figure 9.1 *Relationship of personality type to actual work in formal and informal classrooms*

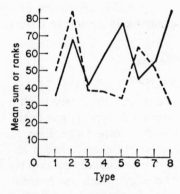

Figure 9.2 *Relationship of personality type to work related pupil interaction in formal and informal classrooms*

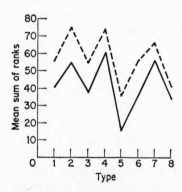

Figure 9.3 *Relationship of personality type to pupil social interaction in formal and informal classrooms*

Figure 9.4 *Relationship of personality type to teacher interaction in formal and informal classrooms*

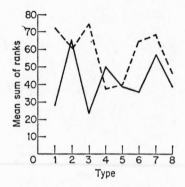

Figure 9.5 *Relationship of personality type to classroom movement in formal and informal classrooms*

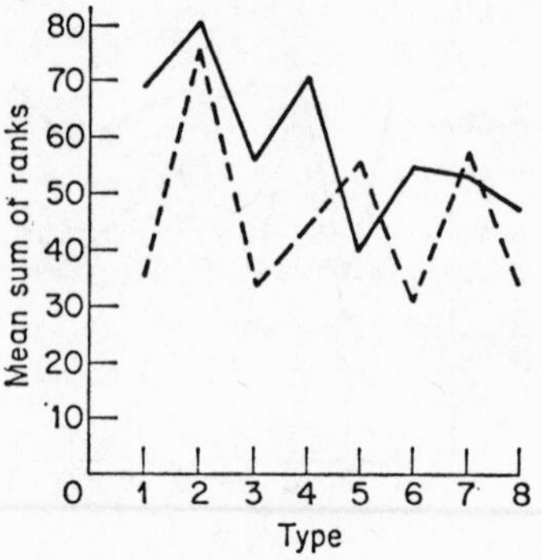

Figure 9.6 *Relationship of personality type to fidgeting in formal and informal classrooms*

Classroom movement

As might be expected, classroom movement is generally greater in informal classrooms. Only among the anxious pupils of type 4 is frequency of movement higher in formal settings, but this difference is small. Grossly disparate patterns are only apparent for the stable extroverts of types 1 and 3 where movement is substantially greater in informal classrooms.

Fidgeting

It will be recalled that fidgeting is more prevalent in formal classrooms, and this is true of all types of pupil except the timid conformists of type 5, but again the difference is slight. There are however some large discrepancies between pupils of the same personality characteristics in different classroom environments. This is particularly so with the stable extroverts of types 1 and 8, who fidget much less in informal classrooms. It will be remembered that these two types of pupil exhibited a high degree of classroom movement in informal settings. It may be that the opportunity to move physically precludes the necessity to fidget. Neurotic introverts fidget the most, irrespective of teaching style.

Negative behaviour

Negative behaviour is more prevalent in informal classrooms, and this is true of most personality types except, surprisingly, the sinners of type 7, who tend to indulge in negative behaviour more often in formal classrooms. The most frequent offenders are the anxious pupils in type 4, and the least frequent the timid conformists.

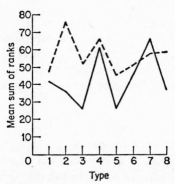

Figure 9.7 *Relationship of personality type to negative behaviour in formal and informal classrooms*

The greatest variation in negative behaviour between the two types of classroom occurs among the neurotic introverts, and to a lesser extent among the stable extroverts of type 3, and the saints. In each case frequency of negative behaviour is much less in formal classrooms.

Full tables of results for all these analyses are presented in appendix F.

SUMMARY

It was stated at the end of chapter 8 that the effect of teaching style was stronger than the effect of pupil personality in relation to attainment. This also seems to be the case in relation to classroom behaviour. In other words the behavioural demands of the situation tend to swamp differences in personality. Nevertheless, in answering the question 'Do pupils of the same personality type behave in similar ways under different teaching styles?' there is evidence to suggest that in many cases the answer is clearly 'no', since only in the category of pupil social interaction are no large discrepancies observed. The major behavioural discrepancies between pupils of the same type who are being taught by different approaches are adumbrated below (see p. 45 for the definition of 'type').

Type 1
This type of pupil exhibits a much greater frequency of work related activity in formal classrooms but less work related interaction. There are extremely large differences in classroom movement and fidgeting, the pupils showing less movement and more fidgeting in formal classrooms and the opposite in informal classrooms.

Type 2
Few differences emerge for pupils in this group. They tend to gossip most in informal classrooms, but more perturbing is the much higher frequency of negative behaviour found among such pupils under informal teaching.

Type 3
These pupils tend to interact more with other pupils in informal settings, but the greatest discrepancies occur in classroom movement, fidgeting and negative behaviour. Movement and negative behaviour are more prevalent in informal classrooms, whereas more fidgeting appears in the formal situation.

Type 4
The feature of greatest concern here is that these pupils were observed to be involved in four times as much work activity in formal as in informal classrooms. They also have a greater frequency of contact with the teacher in the formal setting, together with a higher level of fidgeting.

Type 5
These pupils work less, interact with fellow pupils more, and have less contact with the teacher in informal classrooms. Negative behaviour is more prevalent here also.

Type 6
Few large differences occur for this group although they tend to move less and fidget more in formal classrooms.

Type 7
The self-perceived sinners work less and interact with peers much more frequently under informal teaching. Most of the discrepancies in other behavioural categories are fairly marginal.

Type 8
The self-professed saints work much more, interact far less and enjoy a greater amount of teacher contact in formal classrooms. The extent of negative behaviour is also less in such settings.

INDIVIDUAL PERSONALITY TRAITS AND CLASSROOM BEHAVIOUR

In an attempt to shed more light on the relationship between responses on self report questionnaires and actual behaviour, another set of analyses was carried out relating individual personality scales to categories of classroom behaviour. A number of traits, e.g. extroversion, showed few consistent or significant differences in relation to classroom type, whilst others showed marked, and very similar, discrepancies: these were neuroticism, contentious and fidget.

The level of neuroticism in pupils has a markedly discrepant effect depending upon which type of teacher the pupil finds himself with. In informal classrooms pupils with a high neuroticism score spent half as much time on work activity as those with a lower neuroticism score. They spent more time chatting to other pupils and behaved in a negative manner more frequently. All these differences are significant.

These differences do not appear in formal classes. Level of work activity was as high among neurotic pupils as among their peers with a lower degree of neuroticism. The only significant difference found was that neurotic pupils fidgeted more than pupils with a lower level of neuroticism.

A pupil's level of contentiousness also has different manifestations, depending upon type of teaching. Non-contentious pupils in informal classrooms spent considerably more time on work activities than contentious pupils, and responded more frequently to work related questions put to them by their peers. The contentious pupils spent much more time chatting and behaved badly more frequently. They also gazed into space or looked out of the classroom window more frequently.

In formal classrooms on the other hand contentious pupils worked as frequently as other pupils, although they did tend to interact more with peers.

These same classroom differences were apparent when the fidget trait was examined.

The behavioural manifestations of neuroticism, contentiousness and fidgeting are clearly different in the two types of classroom observed. In each case pupils with these attributes worked less, gossiped more, gazed into space or through the window more, and exhibited more negative behaviour in the classroom under informal teaching, whereas these features were not observed under formal teaching. When these findings are combined with those which show that such pupils progress a good deal less in informal classrooms, one reason why this occurs becomes clear. Unstructured classroom environments where teacher control is less evident do not appear to be ideal for children with this type of personality. It would seem that such children are unable to cope with the responsibility of self-directed activity, and in the absence of teacher-imposed structure often indulge in time-wasting. This is perhaps a salutary message for those who believe that all children at this level of education can adequately cope with self-directed learning strategies.

This chapter was written with the collaboration of Barbara Wade

10

Conclusion

This investigation set out to answer two basic questions which lie at the heart of pedagogic practice: 'Do differing teaching styles result in disparate pupil progress?' and 'Do different types of pupil perform better under certain styles of teaching?' Although no research study is perfect, a number of improvements were incorporated in design, methodology and measurement in order to overcome the perceived inadequacies of previous investigations. These improvements resulted in a clear definition of terms, a more valid typology of teaching styles, a randomly selected sample of teachers, but not of pupils, a wide ranging set of measures for which there is evidence of reasonably high reliability and validity, and a design which allowed the study of possible effects over a reasonable time scale, i.e. one school year.

The creation of the teaching typology required a large scale survey of schools from which it was possible to assess the common belief that informal teaching is relatively widespread, or, as the Plowden Report put it, 'represents a general and quickening trend'. This was not found to be the case in the upper primary school in the geographical area covered by the survey. From the responses of 88 per cent of the 871 schools sampled, a fairly generous estimate is that some 17 per cent of teachers teach in the manner prescribed by Plowden, while at the other end of the teaching continuum approximately one in four teaches formally. The majority of teachers use what have been termed mixed styles, incorporating elements of both formal and informal practice.

It could of course be argued that the schools in the region covered by the survey are not typical of schools in Britain as a whole. There could be some justification in this argument since there are, for example, more church schools in the north-west than elsewhere. But typicality is difficult to define in this context. Teaching methods in Church of England schools, for example, were found to be similar to those in state schools, although those in Roman Catholic schools did tend to be more formal. Similarly there are certain counties in England and Wales whose schools are renowned for their informal ideology, but these too are unlikely to be typical of schools in general.

It is therefore worth noting that other surveys of this kind tend to support the pattern apparent in the north-west. Studies in the west and east Midlands and in Northern Ireland have been carried out, and in the latter it was found that in a 10 per cent sample of the primary schools 'ratings of teaching methods used for mathematics and reading in the upper and lower primary school revealed the majority of teachers as neither formal nor radical in approach but as favouring a mixture of formal practice and practical activities . . . The pupils of all but a few schools were allocated to classes by age and were in ability groups within the class' (Trew 1974). Although not concerned with detailing classroom practice the study lent support to the suggestion of the Northern Ireland Advisory Council for Education that the vast majority of pupils were still being taught by traditional methods.

These findings taken together provide little evidence for a wholesale movement towards informality. But neither do they support the assertion that teachers are moving back towards more formal approaches. The Plowden statement was a subjective, and perhaps hopeful, assessment rather than one based on a comprehensive survey. There are no comparable data on which to base statements about trends. All the data do suggest is that the estimates of writers such as Blackie and Silberman, who assert that some 30 per cent of teachers are following informal approaches, are likely to be optimistic.

In discussing trends in teaching it is obviously important to ascertain what factors influence teachers in their decision to adopt a particular style or approach. This was not investigated in any systematic way but some of the evidence gathered does throw light on this area, particularly the data relating to teaching aims and teacher opinions, and that on the external constraints impinging on the classroom process.

A strong relationship was found between teacher aims and opinions and the way teachers actually teach. This link between aims and methods probably comes as no surprise since it supports other studies, noticeably that by Ashton and others (1975). Teachers aim to engender different outcomes in their pupils. The biggest disagreements about aims occur between formal and informal teachers, with mixed teachers adopting a more middle of the road approach. Formal teachers lay much greater stress on the promotion of a high level of academic attainment, preparation for academic work in the secondary school, and the acquisition of basic skills in reading and number work. Informal teachers on the other hand value social and emotional aims, preferring to stress the importance of self-expression, enjoyment of school and the development of creativity.

These differences in emphasis were again demonstrated in the marked disagreements in opinions about teaching methods. The results, shown fully in chapter 4, illustrate how wide the opinion gap is. Formal teachers defend their methods in entirety and disagree with all the arguments made against them by informal teachers. This is also true of informal teachers, who defend the efficacy of their methods except on the question of discipline, where two-thirds agree that their methods could create discipline problems. On the other hand informal teachers are prepared to concede certain points to formal methods, e.g. that they teach basic skills and concepts effectively, and provide an environment in which pupils are aware of what to do, and minimise time wasting and daydreaming. Formal teachers for their part concede that informal methods are likely to encourage responsibility and self-discipline, and to teach pupils to think for themselves. Mixed teachers, although generally aligning themselves more with formal teachers, agree and disagree with a number of opinions expressed by both.

These results would seem to indicate that aims and opinions are strongly held and that they relate closely to actual classroom practice. They do, however, seem to be mediated to some extent by external factors such as the characteristics of the children taught, the church affiliation of the school, and more powerfully, the presence of the eleven-plus selective examination. The individual effects of these factors are difficult to disentangle since many operate simultaneously, but the eleven-plus was clearly related to a more formal approach. Similarly rural schools tended to be more informal, and Roman Catholic schools more formal.

TEACHING STYLES AND PUPIL PROGRESS

The review of related research had indicated that little difference in progress might be expected under different teaching methods, although there was a suggestion that creativity might be enhanced in informal schools and that reading might be fostered in a more formal environment. These findings are somewhat confounded by poor sampling and the insistence that all teachers can be adequately described by the use of two categories such as progressive and traditional. The Richards and Bolton study on performance in mathematics did seem to indicate that perhaps the middle way was the best way – moderation in all things!

To assess the impact of differing teaching styles on pupil progress, thirty-seven teachers were chosen to represent seven of the twelve teaching styles isolated in the typology. Because of the twin constraints of finance and staffing it was not possible to sample all twelve styles, but the seven chosen adequately represented the full range. The pupils who entered the classroom of these teachers in September 1973 were tested on a wide range of attainment and personality tests on entry, and again the following June. From these data, analyses were computed to ascertain the effect of teaching style across the group of pupils as a whole, on pupils of different sex, on pupils of differing achievement level and on pupils of differing personality type.

The results form a coherent pattern. The effect of teaching style is statistically and educationally significant in all attainment areas tested. In reading, pupils of formal and mixed teachers progress more than those of informal teachers, the difference being equivalent to some three to five months' difference in performance. In mathematics formal pupils are superior to both mixed and informal pupils, the difference in progress being some four to five months. In English formal pupils again out-perform both mixed and informal pupils, the discrepancy in progress between formal and informal being approximately three to five months. It is interesting to note that these differences are very similar to those which have been found in the most recent American research (cf. Solomon and Kendall 1975; Ward and Barcher 1975).

Marked sex differences rarely appear, but differences among pupils of similar initial achievement, but taught by different methods, are often quite marked. In all three attainment areas boys with low achievement on entry to formal classrooms underachieved, i.e. did not progress at the rate expected. This was not true of girls of a similar achievement level, who often overachieved. At the other end of the scale pupils who had entered formal classrooms with a high level of achievement showed much greater progress than pupils of a similar achievement level in informal classrooms. Formal pupils were also superior to their counterparts in mixed classes in mathematics.

These findings will be disturbing to many teachers and parents since they indicate that the teaching approaches advocated by the Plowden Report, and many of the educational advisory staff and college lecturers, often result in poorer academic progress, particularly among high ability children. Concern may also be expressed at the poor performance of low ability boys under formal teaching. It has been noted in other research that formal teaching can result in a widening of the achievement gap between the bright and not so bright pupils. Why this underachievement only occurs in boys is not clear.

The realism of these findings rests heavily on the validity of the measures used. As far as possible the measures chosen were specifically developed to take into account differences in teaching approach. As an added check one third of the teachers taking part in the study were interviewed after the data collection stage to acquire feedback on their perceptions of the conduct of the study. Two questions in the interview schedule are of relevance in this context. The teachers were asked 'Do you think that the attainment tests used were adequate measures of achievement? If not, why?' In reply every teacher thought that they were adequate although one or two felt that the reading test was fairly difficult for low ability pupils. Two teachers remarked that the mathematics test was particularly good in that it really did assess mathematical concepts – 'The children had to think and apply knowledge.'

Also gratifying was the finding that all the teachers said that the results on these tests were in line with what they had expected and tallied well with those from internal tests administered. There was only one exception to this where the scores from the reading test did not match too well those of an internal test in one class.

A common criticism of standardised tests is that they are, in some way, biased against informal teaching. The teachers were therefore asked the question 'Did you feel that the tests showed bias towards either formal or informal types of teaching?' One third felt that there was no bias, one sixth said they were biased towards informal teaching, and the rest that there was some degree of bias towards formal teaching. Some informal teachers felt that the bias was only apparent in the administrative procedures while others felt the bias to be 'very slight', or that it was only apparent in the English test.

The allegation of bias did not all come from informal teachers complaining that the tests favoured formal teaching. The opposite effect was also noted, i.e. formal teachers feeling that the tests might be biased towards informal methods.

In general this feedback would indicate that the teachers were happy with the choice of attainment tests, feeling that they accurately reflected the achievements of their children.

In order to encompass a wider range of pupil attainment, samples of imaginative and descriptive stories were also analysed. These analyses allowed an assessment of the equivocal link between creative writing and informal teaching, and also of the frequently heard criticism that informal teaching tends to depress skills in grammar, punctuation and spelling.

Each script was impression-marked by three teachers, one formal, one mixed and one informal, in order to achieve high reliability in the marking and also to partial out any systematic bias in marking which could be attributed to teaching style.

The findings were not altogether as expected. Girls produced better quality work than boys, a fairly common result among pupils of this age, but no difference was found in either story that could be attributed to a teaching style effect. The pupils in all types of classroom gained very similar marks.

A detailed category schedule was developed to investigate punctuation and spelling errors, and was used to mark the scripts of a matched sample of pupils from the three types of classroom.

The results indicated that the frequency of punctuation errors was much smaller in the written work of formal and mixed pupils than in that of informal pupils. Spelling errors were divided into three categories and here the findings showed sex rather than teaching style disparities. Overall the frequency of spelling errors was slightly higher in the scripts of informal pupils but the differences were marginal.

The evidence suggests that formal and mixed pupils are better at punctuation, and no worse at creative or imaginative writing, than pupils in informal classes. The link between the quality of creative output and informality is not supported whereas that between formality and punctuation skills is. Creativity and formal grammar often seem to be incompatible objectives in the minds of many educationalists, but from this evidence formal and mixed teachers appear to be achieving both.

As an aside it is worth noting how valuable the teachers found marking these scripts. This was spontaneously mentioned by two-thirds of the teachers in the interview. They found it particularly interesting to compare and contrast the work of their own pupils with work from similar classes elsewhere. It made one teacher reappraise her own approach, feeling that she had been 'stressing the creative use of language at the expense of use of imagination'. Primary school teachers rarely gain the opportunity to examine the work of pupils other than those in their own school. This approach might therefore be a useful one for in-service courses. Finally, on the debit side, one teacher criticised the stimulus for the imaginative story which she thought was not exciting enough.

PERSONALITY AND PROGRESS

There is current concern about the effect of open plan schools on certain types of pupil and this concern is echoed in relation to informal teaching. The review of evidence pertaining to this problem clearly pointed to the fact that anxious, insecure children prefer, and perform better in, more structured environments. There was also some evidence that extroverted children cope more easily with less structured situations, and that motivation improves.

The findings on anxiety and motivation were supported in this study, and both showed a similar pattern. Degree of change was as expected in formal classrooms, less than expected in mixed and more than expected in informal classes. Motivation, in the form of attitudes to school and school work, does seem to improve under informal teaching, but at the expense of anxiety which also increases. This increase in anxiety can be interpreted in a number of ways, but perhaps the explanation of greatest theoretical validity is that a more nebulous structure, more often found in informal settings, is not conducive to the needs of many children. Indeed many adults react anxiously when placed in ambiguous situations.

However, the major purpose of the analyses was not to establish links between personality *traits* and academic progress, but to explain the relationships between *types* of pupils and their progress. Pupils who had a similar personality profile were therefore grouped together, producing eight personality types. It was then possible to answer the question 'Do pupils of the same personality type progress at similar rates under differing teaching styles?' The answer is unequivocally 'No.' Differences were noted among all types of pupil but particularly among those groups containing a larger proportion of high achievers, i.e. the motivated stable extroverts (type 1) and the 'saints' (type 8). But similar differences were also evident for the unmotivated stable extroverts (type 3) and motivated neurotics (type 4).

Teaching style clearly has a more powerful effect on progress than pupil personality does, since most pupil types show better progress under formal teaching. The findings presented in chapter 9 provide some explanation as to why this should be, since they highlight the fact that pupils of the same type behave quite differently in formal and informal classrooms. This is particularly noticeable among those pupils whose attributes include a high level of anxiety and neuroticism, who work harder and are more attentive under formal teaching. These findings suggest that formal teaching contains or controls the overt behavioural manifestations of personality whereas informal teaching allows or encourages them. This is no doubt because informal teachers wish to foster self-expression in their pupils, but it should be recognised that this seems to lead to more behaviour which tends to work against effective learning – such as general social gossip, gazing into space or out of the window and various negative behaviours.

It would appear that a number of pupils cannot cope effectively in a less controlled setting, and are unable to accept the responsibility of self directed activity, if indeed they recognise or are told what this responsibility implies. For these pupils a decrease in teacher control often seems to lead to an increase in time wasting.

These results fit neatly into the underlying theoretical model adopted in this study. This model is expounded succinctly by Sells (1973), who argues that the utility of a personality model must be judged on the basis of its capacities to predict and explain behaviour. To do this effectively both the person and the setting in which the person is located must be specified. In Sells's scheme personality represents a unique set of behavioural repertoires consisting of patterns of traits and behaviour in settings, the latter being actual behaviours in the settings in which the person is functioning. He claims that settings limit the behaviours that can occur, and influence their occurrence. It is therefore useless to ascertain personality alone without any details of the setting. This model gains support from the findings presented here since the settings, i.e. formal or informal classrooms, have different influences upon the overt behaviour of pupils with similar personalities. This has obvious connotations for future research on the relationships between personality and school attainment.

MECHANISMS OF PROGRESS

The analyses of the different progress of pupils in the three general teaching styles show clearly the general efficacy of formal methods in the basic subjects. It was felt that these analyses may have been unfair to mixed teaching since this includes a more heterogeneous set of teaching approaches. Analyses were therefore computed for all seven teaching styles sampled, the results of which are less reliable because of smaller sample size. Nevertheless, they indicate that only three of the seven styles were associated with progress above that expected from initial achievement. These were the two formal styles and the mixed style which conjoined a form of integrated day with strict teacher control of content and pupils. Some mixed styles thus appear to be more effective than others.

It is therefore important to attempt to identify those factors within the classroom context which seem to be instrumental in creating these discrepancies in pupil progress. The observation of pupils' behaviour, which unfortunately had to be limited to formal and informal classrooms, provides some evidence on these factors. Pupils in formal classrooms engaged in work related activity much more frequently, the differences being most marked among pupils whose initial achievement level was high. Such children in informal classes engaged in the lowest amount of work related activity, preferring to talk about their work or indulging in purely social interaction. The same general pattern was also true of low achievers in informal classrooms, who engaged in significantly less work than pupils of a similar level in formal situations.

The same pattern also applies when differences in pupil personality are taken into account. All types of pupils engaged in more work activity in formal classrooms. Anxious pupils tended to work less than others but among these large discrepancies were noted in the two types of classroom. The motivated neurotic (type 4) pupils for example were observed to be working four times more often in the formal situation. On the other hand informal pupils interact more both in relation to their work and in general social gossip.

This suggests the juxtaposition low work–low performance in informal classrooms and high work–high performance in formal. Adams (1970a) has argued that 'education is empirically and theoretically bereft', but there is an emerging body of theory relating work activity and attention to academic performance which provides pointers to the likely mechanisms underlying differential pupil progress.

The basic propositions of this theory can be seen in the writings of Rothkopf and Anderson. Rothkopf (1970) contends that 'in most instructional situations what is learned depends largely on the activities of the student.' In other words it depends on the use made by students of the materials and learning experiences provided by the teacher. This accords with Anderson's (1970) general thesis that 'the activities the student engages in when confronted with instructional tasks are of crucial importance in determining what he will learn.' The propositions conform to an earlier model of school learning put forward by Carroll (1963), who contended that, everything else being equal, attainment mastery is determined by the opportunities provided by the teacher for a pupil to study a given content, and the use made of that opportunity by the pupil. This relationship has been investigated by Samuels and Turnure (1974) among six-year-olds, by McKinney and others (1975) among eight-year-olds, by Cobb (1972) among eleven-year-olds and by Lahaderne (1968) among twelve-year-olds. In each study a high correlation was found between work related activity and achievement. McKinney synthesised the findings of these studies and presented a picture of what he called the 'competent child', who is attentive, intelligent and task orientated.

Competence, defined in these terms, is likely to depend on the quality of the teacher–pupil interface since it is much easier for a child to be attentive and task orientated in a classroom in which the teacher imposes an unambiguous structure, as is often the case in formal approaches. In settings where the structure is more inchoate the pupil has the added burden of providing his own structure. Wiley and Harnishfeger (1975) recognise the duality of this effect in a recent paper.

As we conceive it the realities of teaching and learning and the ways in which we structure and understand them are the ways to fundamental policy issues in education. We strongly emphasize the focal role of the pupil and his pursuits as the commonly missing link in a chain mediating all influences on pupil acquisitions. We also stress the teacher as the second vital link. She is the major instrumentality for curriculum implementation.

They, like Carroll, regard time on task as the crucial factor in attainment, their approach deriving from two strong convictions. The first is that 'the total amount of active learning time on a particular instructional topic is *the* most important determinant of pupil achievement on that topic', and the second that 'there is enormous variation in time for learning for different pupils, their time devoted to specific learning topics, and their total amount of active learning time.' They further argue that the investigation of learning time has been neglected – 'the usual fate of the obvious'.

Although this study did not set out to investigate the relationship between work activity and progress the results do, *ex post facto*, fit into this conceptual framework. They suggest that careful and clear structuring of activities together with a curriculum which emphasises cognitive content are the keys to enhanced academic progress. These in fact are the two elements which differentiated the high gain informal classroom from the rest. The teacher was informal in attitude and behaviour, reflecting her type 2 classification (i.e. not the most informal group). But almost half of the classroom activities were on some aspect of English and mathematics, the structuring of which was clear and sequenced. It therefore seems to be curriculum emphasis and organisation rather than classroom organisation factors such as seating, grouping, and degree of movement and talk, which are crucial to pupil performance. This is not to deny that the quality of the environment in which children work is important, merely to suggest that its effect may be relatively marginal in fostering learning. And learning, as Pluckrose (1975), a teacher dedicated to informal teaching, recently pointed out, is still 'the teacher's prime function'.

The relationships found would seem to require a restatement of the obvious – that it is important how pupils spend their time and on what, and what content and learning experiences the teacher provides. The impression gained is that many teachers base their practice on the line of the old song which runs 'It ain't what you do but the way that you do it', but for teaching and learning 'It is what you do, not the way that you do it' would seem more appropriate in the light of this evidence.

The consideration of the mechanisms underlying the superiority of pupil performance in formal classrooms has so far been limited to the behaviour patterns of pupils. These obviously interact with the actions of the teacher and in this context two other explanations are worth considering: firstly the possibility that the results may not reflect badly on informal methods themselves, but on the way these methods are put into practice; secondly – a different possibility – that the results accurately reflect the aims of informal teachers.

It seems generally accepted that to teach well informally is more difficult than to teach well formally. It requires a special sort of teacher to use informal methods effectively – one who is dedicated, highly organised, able to work flexibly, able to plan

ahead and willing to spend a great deal of extra time in prepara-
tory work. How many teachers do we have who could meet these
specifications? Bantock was quoted in chapter 1 as being concerned about this problem, and Burt (1969) also alluded to it in
his critique of informal methods:

With younger children, particularly those drawn from overcrowded
homes in drab surroundings, they [informal methods] have at times
undoubtedly achieved a conspicuous success: the duller pupils are surprisingly happy, and the brighter make remarkable progress. But these
results are exceptional: they are the work of exceptional teachers provided with an exceptional amount of space and equipment – usually
able and ingenious enthusiasts who have themselves devised the techniques they practise. But when copied by the young teacher fresh from
college, the outcome, more often than not, is utter failure.

A supporter of the integrated day sounds the same warning:

The integrated day can be outstandingly successful; and it can be dismally
bad. It is unfortunately a fact that when it does not work the results can
be almost totally unprofitable for the children, and demoralising and
exhausting for the teacher. It is probably no exaggeration to say that
with a more formal structure somebody is almost certain to learn something on the way, whereas with a disorganised Integrated Day it is
perfectly possible for no child to make any real progress at all except
that which comes about more or less by accident. (Taylor 1971)

Burt laid some of the blame on teacher training courses for
substituting for work on teaching methods lectures on the principles of education, 'hammered home by a stock set of clichés and
catchwords'. The education of teachers, like the education of
children, would seem to need much closer examination. One is all
too aware of the fate of the American progressive education
movement when informal methods spread from the hands of the
exceptional teacher in the university laboratory schools to the
average teacher in the state system. It would be a pity if this
extreme reaction were to happen in Britain.

The second explanation is that the poorer academic progress of
informal pupils is an accurate reflection of the aims of informal
teachers. It will be recalled that formal teachers stress academic
aims while informal teachers prefer to stress the importance of
self expression, enjoyment of school and the development of

creativity. These aims are less easy to evaluate both for the teacher and the researcher, but the evidence that can be brought to bear on them would seem to argue that the aims are only partially achieved.

Creative arts were not investigated, but creative or imaginative writing proved to be no better in informal than formal classrooms, although it should be remembered that these data are weaker inferentially than those on academic progress. The aim for greater enjoyment of school does seem to have been fulfilled since attitudes to school and school work did show an improvement over the school year, but this was at the expense of an increase in anxiety.

It is difficult to know what specific outcomes informal teachers intend in developing self-expression. Informal pupils certainly interact more, but the benefits derived from this are not clear from the evidence gathered. Improvements in sociability and self-esteem are no different from those in formal schools, time wasting tends to be manifested more often and there is no academic pay-off, providing some support for the doubtful efficacy of 'learning by talking' commented upon by Froome (1975).

In summary, formal teaching fulfils its aims in the academic area without detriment to the social and emotional development of pupils, whereas informal teaching only partially fulfils its aims in the latter area as well as engendering comparatively poorer outcomes in academic development.

The central factor emerging from this study is that a degree of teacher direction is necessary, and that this direction needs to be carefully planned, and the learning experiences provided need to be clearly sequenced and structured. Experts in the fields of reading and mathematics have recently echoed this same view (Southgate 1973; Biggs 1973). It would seem less than useful for a teacher to stand by and leave a child alone in his inquiries hoping that something will happen. As Bruner (1961) pointed out, 'discovery, like surprise, favours a well prepared mind.'

This study has concentrated on what is rather than what ought to be. The latter is a much more difficult question since there is not, nor is there likely to be, consensus on what should constitute a primary education. Nevertheless it is hoped that the evidence presented will enable a more informed debate on primary school methods to be conducted. It is surely time to ignore the rhetoric which would have us believe that informal methods are pernicious and permissive, and that the most accurate description of formal methods is that found in Dickens's *Hard Times*.

If the key to effective progress lies in the direction and planning provided by teachers, then perhaps another 'ought' is for teachers, and the teachers of teachers, to submit their practices to critical scrutiny. To question critically the bases of one's accepted values and practices can be a disturbing process, but it is an essential one, not only for teachers, but also for the children whose education is the teacher's prime responsibility. In the words of Lady Plowden (1973), 'it is not sufficient to say "this is *what* we do", it is also necessary to know, and to be able to say "this is *why* we do it." It is this deeper understanding which needs to underlie what all teachers do.'

Appendix A

Teacher questionnaire

UNIVERSITY OF LANCASTER

DEPARTMENT OF EDUCATIONAL RESEARCH

SSRC PRIMARY SCHOOL PROJECT

The way in which teachers arrange their classrooms, and methods of teaching adopted, naturally reflect factors such as the conditions under which the school operates, and the characteristics of the pupils. At present all too little is known about the way in which teachers adapt their methods to circumstances, and hence little advice can be passed on to students training to be teachers. In an attempt to obtain information which may be useful in this and other ways, this questionnaire has been devised. It is in three parts, reflecting the attempt to relate circumstances to teaching methods. Thus, part one asks for background information about the teacher, class and school; part two is designed to cover various aspects of classroom and curriculum organisation, and part three asks for teachers' opinions on various educational topics. Additional space is provided at the end of the questionnaire should you wish to elaborate on any of your answers.

For our work to be of any value, we must obtain responses from a wide cross-section of teachers. I hope you will feel that this project is sufficiently worthwhile to merit your support. It generally takes about half an hour to complete the questionnaire, and of course, replies are confidential. It is important in part two that you try to record as objectively as you can what actually happens in your classroom, since student teachers often appear to receive misleading impressions in their training, which later experiences contradict.

Most of the items in this questionnaire ask you to choose one answer from a number of alternatives, by circling the appropriate CODE NUMBER. We realise that this procedure may occasionally involve oversimplification. Other items require a more specific response and you are asked to enter the appropriate figure in the box provided. It is important to answer all questions.

				For Computer Use
PART 1	TEACHER, CLASS AND CLASSROOM.			
PERSONAL DETAILS				1 - 5
1.	Name			
	Name and address of school		Code Number	
	....			
2.	Sex.	Male	0	6
		Female	1	
3.	Age.	Under 30 yrs.	0	
		30 - 39 yrs.	1	
		40 - 49 yrs.	2	7
		50 - 59 yrs.	3	
		Over 60 yrs.	4	
4.	Training.			
	(i) Higher education spent mainly at	University	0	8
		College	1	
	(ii) Qualification	Graduate	0	9
		Non-graduate	1	
	(iii) Formal teacher training	None	0	
		Primary oriented	1	10
		Secondary oriented	2	

			Code Number	For Computer Use
5.	Teaching experience (in years)	Total		11-12
		In primary schools		13-14
		In secondary schools		15-16

CLASS AND CLASSROOM

6.	Number of pupils in class.	Boys		17-18
		Girls		19-20
		Total		21-22

7.	Year group you are teaching.	3rd year Juniors	o	
		4th year Juniors	1	23
		2nd/3rd year mixed	2	
		3rd/4th year mixed	3	

8. If the pupils are streamed by ability, which stream do you teach?

	No streaming	o	
	Stream A	1	
	Stream B	2	24
	Stream C	3	
	Remedial	4	

9.	Approximate area of classroom (in square yards).		25-27

10.	What type of desk is used in the class?		
	Single with seat attached . .	o	
	Single with separate seat . .	1	
	Double with seat attached . .	2	28
	Double with separate seat . .	3	
	Table style seating 3 or more	4	
	Other (please specify). . . .	5	

. . . .

11. Is there a small library or store of books in the classroom?

	No	o	29
	Yes	1	

12. Are there storage facilities in the classroom?

	No	o	30
	Yes	1	

13. Is the heating adequate in the classroom?

	No	o	31
	Yes	1	

14. Is the lighting adequate in the classroom?

	No	o	32
	Yes	1	

	Code Number	For Computer Use

15. What is the level of ability of your pupils?

Mostly bright	0
Bright/average	1
Average	2
Average/dull	3
Mostly dull	4
Full ability range	5

33

PART 2.   TEACHING METHODS ADOPTED   Card II

SEATING ARRANGEMENTS   1 - 5

1. Do your pupils decide for themselves where they sit in the classroom?

No	0
Yes	1

6

2. Are the seats usually arranged so that pupils sit

separately or in pairs? . .	0
in groups of 3 or more? . .	1

7

3. Are pupils allocated to places or groups on the basis of their ability?

No	0
Yes	1

8

4. Do pupils stay in the same seats or groups for most of the day?

No	0
Yes	1

9

CLASSROOM ORGANISATION

5. Do you usually allow your pupils to move around the classroom

generally whenever they wish?	0
only during certain kinds of curricular activity? . . .	1

10

6. Do you usually allow your pupils to talk to one another

usually whenever they wish? .	0
only during certain kinds of curricular activity? . . .	1

11

7. Do you expect your pupils to ask you permission before leaving the room?

No	0
Yes	1

12

8. Do you expect your pupils to be quiet most of the time?

No	0
Yes	1

13

9. Do you appoint monitors with responsibility for certain jobs?

No	0
Yes	1

14

	Code Number	For Computer Use

ORGANISING THE CURRICULUM

10. Do you regularly take pupils out of school as part of your normal teaching activities?

No 0
Yes 1

15

11. Do you use a timetable for organising the week's work?

No 0
Yes 1

16

12. For basic subjects do you more often use

text books? 0
specially prepared materials?. 1

17

13. Do you require that your pupils know their multiplication tables off by heart?

No 0
Yes 1

18

14. Teaching sometimes requires reference materials. Do you normally

supply most of this material for your pupils? 0
ask the pupils to find their own? 1

19

15. Do you regularly give your pupils homework?

No 0
Yes 1

20

16. In organising the work of your class, roughly what emphasis do you give to each of these five different approaches? Indicate approximately what percentage of time is spent on each approach. Your total should come to 100%, although this is not intended to imply that all the work necessarily fits into these five categories.

Percent

1. Teacher talking to the class as a whole. . . . . □

21

2. Pupils working together co-operatively in groups, on work given by the teacher. . . . . □

22

3. Pupils working together co-operatively in groups, on work of their own choice. . . . . □

23

4. Pupils working individually, at their own pace, on work given by the teacher. . . . . □

24

5. Pupils working individually at their own pace, on work of their own choice. . . . . □

25

TOTAL 100% 26-28

17. On which aspect of number work do you place more emphasis?

(i) Developing computational skills through graded exercises? . . . 0
(ii) Exploring concepts with materials or apparatus? 1

29

18. Do you encourage fluency and originality in written English, even if for many children this may be at the expense of grammatical accuracy?

No 0
Yes 1

30

	Code Number	For Computer Use

TESTING AND MARKING

19. Do you put an actual mark or grade on pupils' work?

No 0
Yes 1   31

20. Do you correct most spelling and grammatical errors?

No 0
Yes 1   32

21. Are stars, or their equivalent given to pupils who produce the best work?

No 0
Yes 1   33

22. Do you give your pupils an arithmetic (mental or written) test at least once a week?

No 0
Yes 1   34

23. Do you give your pupils a spelling test at least once a week?

No 0
Yes 1   35

24. Do you have 'end of term' tests?   No 0
Yes 1   36

DISCIPLINE

25. Do you have many pupils who create discipline problems?

No 0
Yes 1   37

26. Do you find verbal reproof and/or reasoning normally sufficient?

No 0
Yes 1   38

27. For persistent disruptive behaviour, where verbal reproof fails to gain the pupils' co-operation, do you use any of the following disciplinary measures?

(i)   extra work   No 0
Yes 1   39

(ii)   smack   No 0
Yes 1   40

(iii) withdrawal of privileges   No 0
Yes 1   41

(iv)   send to head teacher   No 0
Yes 1   42

(v)   sent out of room   No 0
Yes 1   43

Code
Number

For
Computer
Use

ALLOCATION OF TEACHING TIME

28. When time has been deducted for registration and assembly, the
number of hours per week left for teachers is 25. Estimate as
accurately as possible how this is distributed among subjects
and activities in the table below, by putting the appropriate
number of hours in the boxes provided. Please use last week as
your reference unless this was in some way unusual. (for
example, Open day)

Number
of
Hours

Number work . . . .

English (including creative writing).

Reading   44

History . . . .

Geography . . . .

French . . . .

Science (including nature study) . .

Scripture . . . .

P.E. . . . .

Music . . . .

Art and Craft   45

Music and Movement . . . .

Drama . . . .

Environmental Studies . . . .

Social Studies . . . .

Project work . . . .

Free choice activity . . . .

Integrated studies   46

TOTAL   25 (approx.)

PART 3.   OPINIONS ABOUT EDUCATION

Card III

In this section we ask you to give your opinions about a number of educational topics. We are anxious to record the frank opinions of professional teachers and there is no suggestion that there are right or wrong
answers. It is important to answer every question. If you would like
to elaborate on any item please make use of the space provided at the
end of the questionnaire.

1 - 5

TEACHING AIMS

The following are probably all worthwhile teaching aims, but their
relative importance may be influenced by the situation in which the
teacher works. Please rate each aim on the five-point scale to
indicate its importance in relation to your class, by circling the
appropriate code number.

		Not important	Fairly important	Important	Very important	Essential	For Computer Use
				Code Number			
A.	Preparation for academic work in secondary school. .	1	2	3	4	5	6
B.	An understanding of the world in which pupils live.	1	2	3	4	5	7
C.	The acquisition of basic skills in reading and number work.	1	2	3	4	5	8
D.	The development of pupils' creative abilities. . . .	1	2	3	4	5	9
E.	The encouragement of self-expression.	1	2	3	4	5	10
F.	Helping pupils to co-operate with each other. . . .	1	2	3	4	5	11
G.	The acceptance of normal standards of behaviour. . .	1	2	3	4	5	12
H.	The enjoyment of school. . . . . . , ...	1	2	3	4	5	13
I.	The promotion of a high level of academic attainment.	1	2	3	4	5	14

OPINIONS ABOUT EDUCATION ISSUES

Please indicate the strength of your agreement or dis-agreement with the following statements by circling the appropriate code.

		Strongly disagree	Disagree	No opinion	Agree	Strongly agree	
A.	Most pupils in upper junior school have sufficient maturity to choose a topic to study, and carry it through.	1	2	3	4	5	15
B.	Most pupils in upper junior school feel more secure if told what to do and how to do it.	1	2	3	4	5	16
C.	'Creativity' is an educational fad, which could soon die out.	1	2	3	4	5	17
D.	Firm discipline by the teacher leads to good self-discipline on the part of the pupils.	1	2	3	4	5	18
E.	Streaming by ability is undesirable in junior school.	1	2	3	4	5	19
F.	The teacher should be well liked by the class. . . .	1	2	3	4	5	20
G.	Children working in groups waste a lot of time arguing and 'messing about'.	1	2	3	4	5	21
H.	Pupils work better when motivated by marks or stars.	1	2	3	4	5	22
I.	Too little emphasis is placed on keeping order in the classroom nowadays.	1	2	3	4	5	23
J.	Teachers need to know the home background and personal circumstances of their pupils.	1	2	3	4	5	24

OPINIONS ABOUT TEACHING METHODS

To what extent would you agree or disagree with the following statements when
they are applied to (a) FORMAL teaching methods, and (b) INFORMAL teaching
methods?

	a) FORMAL METHODS					b) INFORMAL METHODS					
	Strongly disagree	Disagree	No opinion	Agree	Strongly agree	Strongly disagree	Disagree	No opinion	Agree	Strongly agree	
(i) Could create discipline problems.	1	2	3	4	5	1	2	3	4.	5	25-26
(ii) Fail to bring the best out of bright pupils.	1	2	3	4	5	1	2	3	4	5	27-28
(iii) Make heavy demands on the teacher.	1	2	3	4	5	1	2	3	4	5	29-30
(iv) Encourage responsibility and self-discipline.	1	2	3	4	5	1	2	3	4	5	31-32
(v) Teach basic skills and concepts effectively.	1	2	3	4	5	1	2	3	4	5	33-34
(vi) Encourage time wasting or day-dreaming.	1	2	3	4	5	1	2	3	4	5	35-36
(vii) Leave many pupils unsure of what to do.	1	2	3	4	5	1	2	3	4	5	37-38
(viii) Provide the right balance between teaching and individual work. . . .·. . .	1	2	3	4	5	1	2	3	4	5	39-40
(ix) Allow each child to develop his full potential.	1	2	3	4	5	1	2	3	4	5	41-42
(x) Teach pupils to think for themselves.	1	2	3	4	5	1	2	3	4	5	43-44

THANK YOU FOR COMPLETING THIS QUESTIONNAIRE

*If you would like to make additional comments, or elaborate on answers to our questions, or
to suggest aspects of the classroom we have overlooked, please make use of the space below.
We should be grateful for your comments.*

Appendix B

Teacher aims and opinions: tables of analyses

Teaching style	A 1	A 2	A 3	A 4	A 5	B 1	B 2	B 3	B 4	B 5	C 1	C 2	C 3	C 4	C 5	D 1	D 2	D 3	D 4	D 5	E 1	E 2	E 3	E 4	E 5
1	11	40	43	3	3	0	9	26	49	17	0	0	6	26	69	0	3	20	54	23	0	0	34	34	31
2	13	39	32	13	3	0	0	26	35	39	0	0	13	10	77	0	0	39	39	23	0	3	19	42	35
3	4	17	46	21	13	0	0	38	38	25	0	0	3	13	88	0	3	42	42	17	0	0	29	54	17
4	12	30	36	12	9	0	0	21	27	52	0	0	3	21	76	0	12	33	45	18	0	6	21	42	30
5	12	15	46	19	8	0	11	38	38	23	3	0	4	15	81	0	0	35	35	19	0	8	23	42	27
6	8	19	51	14	8	0	0	38	27	24	0	3	3	24	70	3	3	27	46	27	0	3	32	38	27
7	13	23	40	20	3	3	7	20	27	43	3	0	3	13	80	3	3	40	43	10	0	3	37	37	23
8	3	30	37	10	20	6	0	33	30	33	0	0	3	14	97	3	13	30	37	20	3	14	17	43	17
9	6	19	44	14	17	6	6	31	36	22	3	0	0	3	81	0	14	39	33	14	3	0	37	39	28
10	6	23	55	10	6	3	0	32	35	32	0	0	0	14	84	0	6	45	29	19	0	3	32	48	16
11	0	16	43	22	19	3	5	30	30	32	0	0	0	8	92	0	16	32	43	8	0	6	38	35	11
12	3	9	43	23	23	0	9	26	40	26	0	0	0	20	80	3	3	49	31	14	3	6	43	31	17

Teaching style	F 1	F 2	F 3	F 4	F 5	G 1	G 2	G 3	G 4	G 5	H 1	H 2	H 3	H 4	H 5	I 1	I 2	I 3	I 4	I 5
1	0	3	23	43	31	3	3	37	31	26	3	9	17	26	46	20	37	37	6	0
2	6	0	16	32	45	3	3	16	29	48	0	3	23	35	39	16	19	52	10	3
3	0	6	21	38	42	0	4	13	42	42	0	8	25	38	29	21	8	58	8	4
4	0	6	15	27	52	0	6	21	42	30	0	6	21	39	36	24	30	33	9	3
5	0	4	15	42	38	0	8	19	35	38	4	4	15	38	38	19	4	38	15	0
6	0	5	27	32	35	0	5	35	19	41	0	8	27	30	35	24	19	38	14	5
7	0	3	13	53	30	0	0	35	10	40	0	10	20	30	40	23	27	40	7	3
8	0	3	17	57	23	0	0	20	30	50	0	3	20	50	27	10	30	37	17	7
9	0	6	31	44	25	0	0	11	36	53	0	6	36	42	17	14	28	36	17	6
10	0	6	19	45	29	0	0	10	42	48	3	6	39	35	19	13	39	32	10	6
11	0	5	27	38	30	0	3	24	24	49	3	14	22	43	19	19	22	38	22	0
12	0	3	29	51	17	0	0	20	20	60	3	14	34	29	20	6	23	37	20	14

Key
1 Not important
2 Fairly important
3 Important
4 Very important
5 Essential

Table B.1 *Importance of teaching aims by twelve teaching styles*

Statements / Teaching style	A			B			C			D			E			F			G			H			I			J		
	D	N	A	D	N	A	D	N	A	D	N	A	D	N	A	D	N	A	D	N	A	D	N	A	D	N	A	D	N	A
1	26	6	69	49	3	49	89	9	3	29	23	49	26	9	66	9	17	74	86	3	11	63	20	17	60	14	26	0	0	100
2	55	3	42	13	0	87	87	10	3	39	3	58	13	6	81	3	10	87	65	13	23	61	13	26	55	16	29	0	6	94
3	50	0	50	13	4	83	71	17	13	13	0	88	25	8	67	8	13	79	63	17	21	46	17	38	42	17	42	6	0	96
4	24	3	73	15	12	73	73	18	9	24	15	61	12	6	82	3	12	85	76	12	12	39	12	48	39	3	58	4	0	97
5	50	0	50	19	8	73	77	12	12	23	4	73	27	8	65	0	12	88	81	0	19	62	15	23	50	4	46	3	8	92
6	65	3	32	5	5	89	78	11	11	22	11	68	27	11	62	8	16	76	54	5	41	57	16	27	36	16	51	0	9	92
7	60	3	36	7	7	87	73	13	13	20	10	70	30	10	60	3	17	80	53	17	30	40	37	23	30	17	53	6	3	91
8	53	3	43	10	3	87	53	27	20	0	10	90	40	10	50	7	10	83	40	13	47	20	13	67	20	10	70	7	0	93
9	69	3	28	3	3	94	58	33	8	22	6	72	36	8	56	11	25	64	53	6	42	31	14	56	31	14	56	3	7	90
10	52	0	48	10	0	90	61	26	13	10	10	81	52	13	35	3	16	81	29	13	58	10	16	74	13	6	81	6	3	92
11	51	3	46	8	0	92	73	19	8	14	5	81	30	11	59	11	19	70	32	14	54	19	14	68	19	22	59	3	5	94
12	54	3	23	9	3	89	54	23	23	3	9	89	49	14	37	6	31	63	31	9	60	6	3	91	11	6	83	6	9	86

D = Disagree, N = No opinion, A = Agree

Table B.2 *Opinions about education issues by twelve teaching styles*

(i)

Teaching style	Formal SD	D	N	A	SA	Informal SD	D	N	A	SA
1	9	43	14	32	3	14	23	6	54	3
2	6	32	6	45	10	3	26	3	58	10
3	8	50	8	33	0	4	13	4	75	4
4	18	42	9	30	0	3	12	12	64	9
5	0	46	19	31	4	0	23	4	73	0
6	11	51	14	24	0	0	16	8	65	11
7	23	50	10	17	0	0	7	10	73	3
8	20	53	10	17	0	0	7	7	67	20
9	14	47	17	22	0	3	14	6	64	14
10	23	65	0	13	0	0	13	6	58	23
11	19	59	5	16	0	0	11	3	70	16
12	14	60	11	14	0	0	6	9	77	9

(ii)

Teaching style	Formal SD	D	N	A	SA	Informal SD	D	N	A	SA
1	9	31	6	43	11	11	71	0	14	3
2	0	39	3	48	10	16	58	6	19	0
3	4	50	13	29	4	4	58	8	13	17
4	24	33	16	30	6	12	65	8	12	3
5	4	50	19	19	8	3	65	11	14	4
6	11	54	3	27	5	3	50	17	30	0
7	13	53	7	27	0	7	47	13	27	7
8	23	57	10	10	0	8	47	14	28	0
9	11	61	8	19	0	3	47	13	27	7
10	16	52	13	19	0	3	32	23	19	6
11	11	57	8	24	0	5	35	22	32	5
12	23	54	9	14	0	3	34	17	37	9

(iii)

Teaching style	Formal SD	D	N	A	SA	Informal SD	D	N	A	SA
1	11	63	17	6	3	0	6	3	43	49
2	26	45	3	26	0	0	3	4	39	55
3	13	42	4	29	8	0	4	0	33	63
4	9	48	9	33	0	3	6	3	42	45
5	8	50	8	31	4	0	0	4	54	46
6	3	49	10	35	0	0	11	3	54	35
7	7	50	17	33	0	3	7	3	47	43
8	7	47	6	33	7	0	6	3	50	43
9	3	50	6	33	8	0	6	3	50	42
10	3	32	13	42	10	0	3	5	42	48
11	3	32	24	32	8	3	3	5	41	49
12	11	26	14	40	9	3	9	3	43	46

(iv)

Teaching style	Formal SD	D	N	A	SA	Informal SD	D	N	A	SA
1	20	60	17	3	0	0	3	3	54	40
2	19	35	19	26	0	0	6	10	58	26
3	8	21	21	46	4	0	13	6	58	21
4	6	39	3	48	3	0	0	6	64	18
5	12	46	19	23	0	0	12	8	73	8
6	3	51	19	24	3	7	17	19	62	3
7	3	23	27	40	7	3	17	17	57	3
8	0	20	17	53	10	3	20	23	43	10
9	3	42	19	28	8	3	19	14	58	6
10	0	23	19	48	10	3	16	23	52	6
11	0	24	14	62	0	3	27	14	57	0
12	0	9	31	54	6	3	23	29	40	6

(v)

Teaching style	Formal SD	D	N	A	SA	Informal SD	D	N	A	SA
1	3	17	9	69	3	0	17	11	63	9
2	3	29	3	58	6	0	16	10	71	3
3	6	36	8	58	25	0	33	21	46	0
4	0	23	12	65	0	9	55	18	18	0
5	0	0	5	62	24	0	23	19	54	4
6	3	7	5	62	27	8	27	19	46	0
7	0	0	0	57	40	10	47	13	30	0
8	0	6	14	61	19	27	30	17	27	0
9	0	0	3	61	32	6	39	25	31	0
10	0	0	3	62	32	6	58	16	16	3
11	0	0	9	49	43	14	49	27	14	0
12	0	0	9	49	43	14	49	23	14	0

(vi)

Teaching style	Formal SD	D	N	A	SA	Informal SD	D	N	A	SA
1	3	51	20	23	3	0	77	3	20	0
2	0	52	26	19	3	0	52	16	32	0
3	0	63	13	17	0	4	21	17	46	13
4	0	52	12	33	0	0	50	19	31	0
5	4	69	19	8	0	3	32	16	41	8
6	4	65	14	14	3	3	13	17	57	10
7	27	50	10	13	10	3	23	7	53	17
8	17	53	7	3	10	3	22	14	53	8
9	17	61	14	8	0	3	19	10	52	19
10	23	68	6	3	0	5	16	11	57	11
11	19	70	11	0	0	0	11	14	60	14
12	26	60	11	3	0	0	11	14	60	14

SD = Strongly disagree, D = Disagree, N = No opinion, A = Agree, SA = Strongly agree

Table B.3 *Opinions about teaching methods by twelve teaching styles*

(vii)

Teaching style	Formal					Informal				
	SD	D	N	A	SA	SD	D	N	A	SA
1	9	66	14	11	0	0	51	37	11	0
2	6	61	10	19	3	4	48	13	39	0
3	13	79	4	4	0	4	29	8	42	17
4	6	61	9	24	0	0	39	9	45	6
5	4	69	12	12	4	3	38	15	42	4
6	5	70	14	11	0	3	30	14	46	8
7	13	77	3	7	0	0	10	7	70	13
8	30	53	7	10	0	0	27	10	33	30
9	14	72	8	6	0	0	31	6	50	14
10	26	68	3	3	0	0	8	11	71	23
11	27	68	5	6	0	3	8	11	54	24
12	23	66	6	6	0	0	6	11	63	20

(viii)

Teaching style	Formal					Informal				
	SD	D	N	A	SA	SD	D	N	A	SA
1	11	54	17	14	3	0	6	9	63	23
2	16	39	13	32	0	0	3	13	68	16
3	13	29	17	29	13	4	25	25	42	4
4	9	39	21	24	6	0	21	18	55	6
5	8	58	12	31	0	0	12	12	65	12
6	8	38	16	35	3	0	22	19	57	3
7	0	23	17	53	7	3	37	20	37	3
8	0	13	13	63	10	3	30	23	43	0
9	3	25	28	39	8	0	33	25	36	6
10	3	10	23	45	19	0	29	45	23	3
11	0	8	22	62	8	3	38	35	24	0
12	0	9	29	40	23	0	40	43	17	0

(ix)

Teaching style	Formal					Informal				
	SD	D	N	A	SA	SD	D	N	A	SA
1	14	69	9	9	0	0	0	9	57	34
2	29	42	10	19	0	0	13	10	55	23
3	13	29	21	33	4	4	13	25	54	4
4	9	33	18	36	3	0	18	15	55	12
5	12	58	8	23	0	0	23	15	54	8
6	5	51	19	22	3	6	22	16	54	8
7	7	33	14	43	3	6	23	13	57	0
8	0	17	20	53	10	7	33	23	37	0
9	6	39	14	39	8	7	28	17	44	8
10	6	23	23	19	10	0	35	34	26	3
11	0	24	22	54	0	3	24	30	41	3
12	0	20	9	63	9	3	49	23	26	0

(x)

Teaching style	Formal					Informal				
	SD	D	N	A	SA	SD	D	N	A	SA
1	26	60	9	6	0	0	6	6	43	46
2	32	35	13	19	0	0	3	13	42	42
3	8	33	21	29	8	0	4	13	67	17
4	6	42	24	24	3	0	0	13	76	12
5	15	54	4	27	0	0	8	4	77	12
6	3	43	24	27	3	0	5	16	65	14
7	10	23	20	40	7	3	10	20	60	7
8	0	13	17	63	7	3	13	10	70	3
9	0	39	25	31	6	0	11	17	61	11
10	3	23	29	39	6	0	3	26	68	3
11	3	24	24	51	0	0	8	16	70	5
12	3	17	26	46	9	0	11	26	57	6

SD = Strongly disagree, D = Disagree, N = No opinion, A = Agree, SA = Strongly agree

Table B.3 (continued)

Appendix C

Sample details and analyses of covariance

The teacher sample was chosen to be representative of the teaching styles identified. There was also control for other factors. For example, there were no significant differences between formal and informal teachers in age range, sex, teaching experience, size of class taught, or age of school buildings. However, the pupil sample was composed of those children who happened to be allocated to those teachers chosen.

Analyses of change were computed for the 950 pupils for whom information was available on all measures at pre- and post-test. The mean scores and standard deviations for all attainment measures are shown in table C.1. From this table it can be seen that formal pupils showed higher initial achievement, necessitating an analysis which took these differences into account.

Analyses of covariance were undertaken after homogeneity of regression had been established. These were computed at the University of Newcastle Computer Centre by John Leece. Tables C.2, C.3 and C.4 present details of these analyses separately for reading, mathematics and English.

| | Reading | | | | Mathematics | | | | English | | | | Analysis sample |
| | Pre-test | | Post-test | | Pre-test | | Post-test | | Pre-test | | Post-test | | |
	Mean	s.d.	Mean	s.d.	Mean	s.d.	Mean	s.d.	Mean	s.d.	Mean	s.d.	
Formal	103·2	14·3	109·1	14·0	102·2	13·2	108·5	14·9	105·6	13·9	111·5	13·1	335
Mixed	96·3	15·7	104·5	14·5	95·7	12·9	99·2	13·9	97·8	14·6	103·8	12·3	294
Informal	98·0	15·8	103·2	14·3	97·5	13·1	101·8	14·0	99·5	14·1	104·3	13·4	321

Table C.1 Pre- and post-test attainment scores by teaching style

Sources	SS	df	MS	F	P
Initial achievement	136341·88	1	136341·88	2089·17	0·001
Teaching style	1034·00	2	517·00	7·92	0·001
Residual	61802·56	947	65·26		
Total	199178·44	950	209·66		

Table C.2 *Analysis of covariance: reading by teaching style and initial achievement*

Source	SS	df	MS	F	p
Initial achievement	144134·56	1	144134·56	2152·46	0·001
Teaching style	1866·05	2	933·03	13·93	0·001
Residual	63413·81	947	66·96		
Total	209414·44	950	220·43		

Table C.3 *Analysis of covariance: mathematics by teaching and initial achievement*

Source	SS	df	MS	F	p
Initial achievement	118945·69	1	118945·69	2141·56	0·001
Teaching style	1095·44	2	547·72	9·86	0·001
Residual	52598·00	947	55·54		
Total	172639·13	950	181·73		

Table C.4 *Analysis of covariance: English by teaching style and initial achievement*

Appendix D

Pupil behaviour: tables of analyses

	Median scores			Mann–Whitney U Test	
Activity	Total sample	Formal (23)	Informal (9)	U	p (1 tailed)
Preparation	8·5	6	10	71·0	0·09
Waiting	1·0	0	1	101·0	0·46
Miscellaneous	18·5	14	17	98·5	0·42
Writing	21·5	25	19	83·5	0·20
Computation	21·5	35	28	74·0	0·11
Making	16·0	16	9	72·5	0·10
Reading	10·0	16	14	101·5	0·47
Total work	109·0	121	110	52·5	0·02*
Actual work	96·0	110	86	47·5	0·009†

$$* p < 0.05 \quad † p < 0.01$$

Table D.1 *Median scores for work activity for high achieving pupils in formal and informal classrooms*

	Median scores			Mann–Whitney U Test	
Activity	Total sample	Formal (16)	Informal (18)	U	p (1 tailed)
Preparation	8·5	11·5	8·5	105·0	0·09
Waiting	1·0	2·0	2·0	140·0	0·45
Miscellaneous	18·5	6·0	19·5	55·0	0·001†
Writing	21·5	21·5	21·0	139·0	0·43
Computation	21·5	32·0	21·0	90·5	0·03*
Making	16·0	24·0	22·0	134·0	0·36
Reading	10·0	14·5	9·5	134·5	0·37
Total work	109·0	112·5	110·5	136·0	0·39
Actual work	96·0	97·5	96·0	138·5	0·42

$$* p < 0.05 \quad † p < 0.01$$

Table D.2 *Median scores for work activity for average achieving pupils in formal and informal classrooms*

Activity	Median scores			Mann–Whitney U Test	
	Total sample	Formal (9)	Informal (26)	U	p (1 tailed)
Preparation	8·5	8·0	9·5	117·0	0·5
Waiting	1·0	1·0	2·0	80·5	0·09
Miscellaneous	18·5	22·0	16·0	111·0	0·41
Writing	21·5	33·0	20·5	99·0	0·25
Computation	21·5	12·0	15·0	113·5	0·45
Making	16·0	4·0	14·0	102·5	0·29
Reading	10·0	16·0	9·0	83·5	0·10
Total work	109·0	110·0	98·5	44·5	0·003*
Actual work	96·0	99·0	84·5	42·5	0·003*

*p < 0·01

Table D.3 *Median scores for work activity for low achieving pupils in formal and informal classrooms*

Activity	Median scores			Mann–Whitney U Test	
	Total sample (101)	Formal (23)	Informal (9)	U	p (1 tailed)
Asking	3·0	4·0	2·0	100·0	0·44
Responding	3·0	3·0	3·0	95·5	0·37
Cooperating	13·0	9·0	14·0	50·0	0·01†
Attracting attention	0·5	1·0	2·0	75·5	0·12
Play/chat	10·0	5·0	12·0	57·0	0·03*
Negative/ argumentative	0·0	0·0	1·0	93·0	0·33
Total interaction	36·0	24·0	46·0	45·5	0·008†
Work interaction	22·5	17·0	23·0	62·5	0·04*
Social interaction	12·0	6·0	14·0	55·5	0·02*

*p < 0·05   †p < 0·01

Table D.4 *Median scores for pupil interaction for high achieving pupils in formal and informal classrooms*

Activity	Median scores Total sample (101)	Formal (16)	Informal (18)	Mann–Whitney U Test U	p (1 tailed)
Asking	3·0	3·5	3·0	127·0	0·28
Responding	3·0	6·5	4·5	104·5	0·09
Cooperating	13·0	16·0	14·5	130·0	0·32
Attracting attention	0·5	0·5	0·0	117·5	0·18
Play/chat	10·0	11·0	8·5	120·0	0·21
Negative/ argumentative	0·0	1·0	0·5	122·0	0·22
Total interaction	36·0	37·5	33·5	131·5	0·33
Work interaction	22·5	27·0	24·0	129·5	0·31
Social interaction	12·0	12·5	12·0	118·0	0·18

Table D.5 *Median scores for pupil interaction for average achieving pupils in formal and informal classrooms*

Activity	Median scores Total sample	Formal (9)	Informal (26)	Mann–Whitney U Test U	p (1 tailed)
Asking	3·0	4·0	4·0	98	0·24
Responding	3·0	4·0	4·0	112	0·42
Cooperating	13·0	14·0	16·0	98	0·24
Attracting attention	0·5	1·0	1·0	101	0·27
Play/chat	10·0	11·0	13·0	71	0·04*
Negative/ argumentative	0·0	0·0	1·5	75	0·06
Total interaction	36·0	40·0	44·0	77	0·07
Work interaction	22·5	21·0	27·5	95	0·21
Social interaction	12·0	13·0	17·0	74	0·05*

*p < 0·05

Table D.6 *Median scores for pupil interaction for low achieving pupils in formal and informal classrooms*

Level of initial achievement	Activity	Median scores			Mann–Whitney U Test	
		Total sample	Formal	Informal	U	p (1 tailed)
High	Responding	4	7 (23)	3 (9)	66·5	0·06
	Total interaction	9	10	5	63·5	0·05 *
Average	Responding	4	4 (16)	3 (18)	128·5	0·29
	Total interaction	9	9.5	7	140·5	0·45
Low	Responding	4	3 (9)	2 (26)	102·5	0·29
	Total interaction	9	11	7·5	114	0·46

Table D.7 *Median scores for teacher interaction for pupils of three achievement levels in formal and informal classrooms*

Level of initial achievement	Total sample	Median scores		Mann–Whitney U Test	
		Formal	Informal	U	p (1 tailed)
High	29	33	27	85	0·22
Average	29	30·5	25·5	103·5	0·08
Low	29	32	23·5	57·5	0·01*

*p < 0·05

Table D.8 *Median scores for watching teacher for pupils of three achievement levels in formal and informal classrooms*

Level of initial achievement	Total sample	Median scores		Mann–Whitney U Test	
		Formal	Informal	U	p (1 tailed)
High	22	25 (23)	18 (9)	67	0·06
Average	22	21 (16)	24.5 (18)	135	0·38
Low	22	40 (9)	21.5 (26)	75	0·06

Table D.9 *Median scores for watching pupils for pupils of three achievement levels in formal and informal classrooms*

Level of initial achievement	Total sample	Median scores		Mann–Whitney U Test	
		Formal	Informal	U	p (1 tailed)
High	8·5	6 (23)	7 (9)	77	0·13
Average	8·5	9 (16)	10 (18)	103·5	0·08
Low	8·5	10 (9)	13 (9)	83	0·10

Table D.10 *Median scores for classroom movement for pupils of three achievement levels in formal and informal classrooms*

Level of initial achievement	Total sample	Median scores		Mann–Whitney U Test	
		Formal	Informal	U	p (1 tailed)
High	42	46 (23)	30 (9)	40·5	0·004†
Average	42	45·5 (16)	37·5 (18)	78·5	0·05*
Low	42	52 (9)	43 (26)	78·5	0·07

*p < 0·05   † p < 0.01

Table D.11 *Median scores for fidgeting for pupils of three achievement levels in formal and informal classrooms*

Appendix E

Children's writing: tables of analyses

Teachers	1	2	3	4	
Informal 1	—				
Mixed 2	0·63	—			Imaginative story
Formal 3	0·62	0·65	—		
Overall 4	0·86	0·86	0·86	—	
Informal 1	—				
Mixed 2	0·58	—			Descriptive story
Formal 3	0·66	0·56	—		
Overall 4	0·89	0·72	0·88	—	

Table E.1 *Inter-marker correlations*

Punctuation	PC	PF	PFa	Pa	PG	PGA	PK	Pd	PO	Total
Whole sample	9·8	5·4	1·4	0·3	0·3	0·3	2·7	2·4	0·5	23·8
Formal boys	9·1	4·8	1·0	0·6	0·2	0·1	2·2	1·5	0·3	19·4
Formal girls	7·6	4·8	1·1	0·5	0·3	0·1	2·7	2·2	0·3	19·5
Mixed boys	9·5	5·4	1·2	0·3	0·3	0·2	1·7	1·8	0·4	20·5
Mixed girls	9·0	5·0	1·4	0·3	0·5	0·4	2·3	2·2	1·1	22·4
Informal boys	12·9	6·8	1·8	0·1	0·4	0·7	3·2	3·4	0·3	29·6
Informal girls	10·9	5·7	1·6	0·3	0·4	0·2	4·1	3·3	0·2	31·3

The difference between formal and informal is significant at the 0·05 level.

Table E.2 *Punctuation errors by sex and teaching style*

Phonetic misspelling	PH	PHC	PHG	PHU	PHA	Total
Whole sample	5·9	1·1	1·4	1·3	0·1	9·0
Formal boys	6·0	0·9	1·1	2·2	0·3	10·3
Formal girls	4·1	1·2	1·1	1·9	0·2	8·0
Mixed boys	7·5	1·0	1·2	1·2	0	8·8
Mixed girls	5·5	1·5	1·4	1·1	0	9·0
Informal boys	7·2	1·2	1·3	1·1	0·1	10·9
Informal girls	5·1	0·8	2·1	0·3	0·1	6·8

Table E.3 *Phonetic misspellings by sex and teaching style*

Misspelling by analogy	AR	AE	AI	AT	Total
Whole sample	0·8	0·3	0	0·1	1·2
Formal boys	0·7	0·2	0	0·2	1·1
Formal girls	0·6	0·3	0	0	1·0
Mixed boys	0·9	0·4	0	0	1·2
Mixed boys	0·4	0·2	0	0·1	0·6
Informal boys	1·1	0·3	0	0·1	1·6
Informal girls	0·9	0·4	0·1	0·1	1·5

Differences between formal and informal, and between mixed and informal, are significant at the 0·05 level.

Table E.4 *Misspellings by analogy by sex and teaching style*

Carelessness	C	CI	I	MW	CG	CO	Total
Whole sample	0·2	0·2	0·1	0·8	1·1	0·1	2·3
Formal boys	0·1	0·1	0·2	0·8	0·7	0	2·0
Formal girls	0	0·2	0·1	0·8	0·9	0	1·8
Mixed boys	0·3	0·2	0	0·7	1·6	0·1	2·8
Mixed girls	0·2	0·3	0·1	0·8	1·4	0·1	2·9
Informal boys	0·1	0·2	0·1	0·9	1·1	0·4	2·5
Informal girls	0·1	0·1	0	0·7	0·8	0·1	1·7

Table E.5 *Carelessness by sex and teaching style*

Appendix F

Pupil personality and classroom behaviour: tables of analyses

	Pre-test means	Post-test means	Test-retest reliability (6 weeks)	Test-retest reliability (8 months)	Alpha
Extroversion[1]	18·6	19·1	N/A	0·53	—
Neuroticism[1]	11·3	8·7	N/A	0·62	—
Psychoticism[1]	3·3	3·4	N/A	0·58	—
Lie[1]	9·5	9·1	N/A	0·54	—
Contentious	43·6	46·2	0·80	0·68	0·83
Sociability	22·5	24·4	0·80	0·58	0·77
Attitude to school	36·6	35·5	0·74	0·68	0·68
Fidget/ distractability	37·2	37·9	0·72	0·64	0·80
Self evaluation	34·2	33·8	0·52	0·48	0·52
Anxiety	49·6	47·1	0·79	0·64	0·89
Motivation	91·0	86·1	0·71	0·64	0·79
Academic self image[2]	18·1	19·3	N/A	0·54	—
Unsociability[2]	12·9	14·0	N/A	0·49	—
Introversion[2]	14·6	14·1	N/A	0·49	—
Conformity[2]	18·9	18·2	N/A	0·44	—

[1] Eysenck's Junior Personality Questionnaire
[2] Semantic differential

Table F.1 *Mean scores and reliability estimates for traits measured*

Behaviour category	Mean sum of ranks Pupil cluster								H	p
	1 (16)	2 (4)	3 (12)	4 (18)	5 (8)	6 (21)	7 (12)	8 (10)		
Preparation	53·6	36·3	49·7	54·4	42·8	46·9	64	48·1	4·9	n.s.
Miscellaneous	48·6	52·8	61·2	46·3	81·3	45·6	37·4	53·7	14·0	n.s.
Writing	58·3	43·3	24·6	51·8	50·7	60·4	47·4	57·5	13·9	n.s.
Computation	54·9	42·3	46·8	40·9	41·6	61·6	57·6	48·9	7·2	n.s.
Making	55	44·9	73·9	49	40·6	44·8	46·3	50·2	10·2	n.s.
Reading	43·2	50·8	65·4	52·3	54·1	46·2	32	50·4	4·7	n.s.
Waiting to see teacher	48	66·5	53·3	38·7	66·6	54·4	50·8	49·6	7·2	n.s.
Total work	48	34·8	66·5	42·1	60·3	51·7	49·9	50·7	7·1	n.s.
Actual work	51	28·8	66·3	42·3	58·8	54·5	44·3	51·8	8·7	n.s.

Table F.2 *Kruskal–Wallis one-way analyses of variance of the behaviour of pupils of different types: work activity*

Behaviour category	Mean sum of ranks Pupil cluster								H	p
	1 (16)	2 (4)	3 (12)	4 (18)	5 (8)	6 (21)	7 (12)	8 (10)		
Asking	54·5	44·5	44·5	48·2	42·1	56·9	52·8	53·5	2·9	n.s.
Responding	58·8	36·6	38·9	54·1	45·3	57·5	38·4	59·3	8·7	n.s.
Cooperating	47·4	57·8	57·5	42·8	43·6	60·9	49·5	47·9	5·5	n.s.
Attracting attention	54·2	56·9	61·2	49·8	32	50·2	48·6	53·3	5·4	n.s.
Play/chat	51·5	68·1	48·9	64·5	28·8	44·6	63·5	37·8	15·1	*
Total pupil interaction	52·6	53·4	51·3	54·1	32·1	54	54·7	46	4·3	n.s.
Work interaction	51·5	50·1	55·7	43·4	39·8	61·4	46·5	50·7	5·6	n.s.
Social interaction	50·1	65·8	49·5	66·3	26·6	45·1	63·1	38·4	16·3	*

*$p > 0.05$

Table F.3 *Kruskal–Wallis one-way analyses of variance of the behaviour of pupils of different types: pupil interaction*

Behaviour category	Mean sum of ranks Pupil cluster								H	p
	1 (16)	2 (4)	3 (12)	4 (18)	5 (8)	6 (21)	7 (12)	8 (10)		
Asking	48·3	66·3	51·6	52·1	43	54·5	52·8	43·6	2·8	n.s.
Responding	45·4	74·8	48·9	53·1	53·9	49·5	43·7	58·7	4·9	n.s.
Cooperating	51·9	49·5	36·7	46·1	54·6	57·7	68·8	37·8	11·1	n.s.
Attracting attention	45·4	65·6	36·5	50·8	48·8	63·4	47	54·6	8·3	n.s.
Play/chat	51·8	66	56	46·7	59·3	48·5	47·5	48·2	2·8	n.s.
Total teacher interaction	44	76·5	40·6	50·5	55·8	53·6	53·5	53·1	6·1	n.s.

Table F.4 *Kruskal–Wallis one-way analyses of variance of the behaviour of pupils of different types: teacher interaction*

Behaviour category	Mean sum of ranks Pupil cluster								H	p
	1 (16)	2 (4)	3 (12)	4 (18)	5 (8)	6 (21)	7 (12)	8 (10)		
Negative behaviour	45·4	55·3	44·1	63·1	36·1	48·7	61	49·5	8·0	n.s.
Watching teacher	54·7	40·9	39·9	55·1	64·9	48·7	48·9	51·2	4·8	n.s.
Watching pupils	50	26·4	43·8	65·8	62·9	47·2	51·1	42·6	10·5	n.s.
Avoidance	47·8	50·6	56·1	48	46·1	55·9	60·5	37·9	4·8	n.s.
Classroom movement	52·8	63·1	57·8	45·1	39·3	48·4	64·6	44·3	6·7	n.s.
Fidget	50·8	78·9	42·7	58·6	48·3	45·3	55·9	44·8	7·4	n.s.

Table F.5 *Kruskal–Wallis one-way analyses of variance of the behaviour of pupils of different types: other activities*

References *and* Name index

ADAMS, R. S. (1970a) 'Perceived teaching styles', *Comparative Education Review* (February 1970), 50–9 *39–40, 158*

ADAMS, R. S. (1970b) 'The classroom context', in Campbell, W. J. (ed.) *Scholars in Context* (Wiley, Sydney) *129*

ADAMS R. S. (1972) 'Observational studies of teacher role', *International Review of Education* 18, 440–59 *30–1*

ANDERSON, H. H. (1939) 'The measurement of dominative and socially integrative behaviour in teachers' contacts with children', *Child Development* 10, 73–89 *14, 18*

ANDERSON, R. C. (1959) 'Learning in discussions: a resumé of the authoritarian–democratic studies', *Harvard Educational Review* 29, 201–15 *13*

ANDERSON, R. C. (1970) 'Control of student mediating processes during verbal learning and instruction', *Review of Educational Research* 40, 349–69 *158*

ARGYLE, M. and LITTLE, B. R. (1972) 'Do personality traits apply to social behaviour?', *Journal of Theory and Social Behaviour* 2, 1–35 *128*

ASHTON, P., KNEEN, P., DAVIES, F. and HOLLEY, B. J. (1975) *The Aims of Primary Education: A Study of Teachers' Opinions* (Macmillan, London) *63, 67, 78, 150*

AUSUBEL, D. P. (1963) *The Psychology of Meaningful Verbal Learning* (Grune and Stratton, New York) *37*

BALDWIN, C. P. (1965) 'Naturalistic studies of classroom learning', *Review of Educational Research* 35, 107–13 *13*

BANTOCK, G. H. (1969) 'Discovery methods', in Cox and Dyson (1969b) *6, 161*

BARKER LUNN, J. C. (1970) *Streaming in the Primary School* (N.F.E.R., Slough) *26–7, 55, 58, 81*

BARR, A. S. and EMANS, L. M. (1930) 'What qualities are pre-requisite to success in teaching?', *Nations Schools* 6, 30–4 *12*

BARTH, R. S. (1972) *Open Education and the American School* (Agathon Press, New York) *8, 40*

BELLACK, A., KLIEBARD, H. M., HYMAN, R. T. and SMITH, F. L. (1966) *The Language of the Classroom* (Teachers College Press, Columbia University) *18*

BENNETT, S. N. (1972) 'The relationships between personality, divergent thinking abilities and academic attainment in ten to twelve year old schoolchildren', unpublished Ph.D. thesis (University of Lancaster) *117*

BENNETT, S. N. (1973a) 'A re-evaluation of the Junior Eysenck Personality Inventory'. *British Journal of Educational Psychology* 43, 131–9 *128*

BENNETT, S. N. (1973b) 'Divergent thinking abilities – a validation study', *British Journal of Educational Psychology* 43, 1–7 *117*

BENNETT, S. N. (1974) 'Plowden's progress: informal one in six', *Times Educational Supplement*, 18 October 1974, 21 *7*

BENNETT, S. N. (1975) 'Cluster analysis in educational research', *Research Intelligence* 1, 64–70 *45*

BENNETT, S. N. and JORDAN, J. (1975) 'A typology of teaching styles in primary schools', *British Journal of Educational Psychology* 45, 20–8 *45*

BENNETT, S. N. and YOUNGMAN, M. B. (1973) 'Personality and behaviour in school', *British Journal of Educational Psychology* 43, 228–33 *128–9*

BERLINER, D. C. and CAHEN, L. S. (1973) 'Trait-treatment interaction and learning', in Kerlinger, F. N. (ed.) *Review of Research in Education* (Peacock, Itasca, Ill.) *24*

BEST, K. G. (1973) 'Children's situational responses to the Junior Eysenck Personality Inventory', unpublished M.A. thesis (University of Lancaster) *128*

BIGGS, E. E. (1973) 'Forward and back', *Education* 3–13, 1, 83–7 *162*

BLACKIE, J. (1967) *Inside the Primary School* (H.M.S.O., London) *54, 150*

BLOOM, B. S. (1972) 'Innocence in education', *School Review* 80, 333–52 *1*

BOBBITT, F. (1924) *How to Make a Curriculum* (Houghton Mifflin, Boston *2*

BRACHT, G. H. (1970) 'Experimental factors related to aptitude–treatment interactions', *Review of Education Research* 40, 627–45 *24*

BRACHT, G. H. and GLASS, G. V. (1968) 'The external validity of experiments', *American Educational Research Journal* 5, 437–74 *24*

BRANDT, A. M. (1972) *Studying Behaviour in Natural Settings* (Holt, Rinehart and Winston, New York) *14*

BRITTON, J. (1972) 'What's the USE: a schematic account of language functions', *Educational Review* 23, 205–19 *120–1*

BRITTON, J., MARTIN, N. C. and ROSEN, H. (1966) *Multiple Marking of English Composition*, Schools Council Examination Bulletin 12 (Evans/Methuen, London) *121, 124*

BRUNER, J. S. (1961) 'The act of discovery', *Harvard Educational Review* 31, 21–32 *37, 162*

BULLOCK REPORT (1975) *A Language for Life* (H.M.S.O., London) *81–3, 116, 121*

BURT, C. (1969) 'The mental differences between children', in Cox and Dyson (1969b), 1–7 *161*

BUSSIS, A. M. and CHITTENDEN, E. A. (1970) 'Analysis of an approach to open education', report to Princeton N.J. Education Testing Service *40*

CALVIN, A. D., HOFFMAN, F. K. and HARDEN, E. L. (1957) 'The effect of intelligence and social atmosphere on group problem solving behaviour', *Journal of Social Psychology* 45, 61–74 *19*

CARROLL, J. B. (1963) 'A model of school learning', *Teachers College Record* 64, 723–33 *24, 159*

COBB, J. A. (1972) 'Relationship of discrete classroom behaviours to fourth grade academic achievement', *Journal of Educational Psychology* 63, 74–80 *103, 159*

COX, C. B. and DYSON, R. E. (eds) (1969a) *Black Paper I – Fight for Education*

(1969b) *Black Paper II – The Crisis in Education* (1970) *Black Paper III – Goodbye Mr Short* (The Critical Quarterly Society, London); (1975) *Black Paper 1975 – The Fight for Education* (Dent, London) *5–6*

CREBER, P. (1966) *Sense and Sensitivity* (University of London Press, London) *115*

CRONBACH, L. J. (1966) 'The logic of experiments on discovery', in Shulman and Keislar (1966) *1, 28, 34*

CRONBACH, L. J. and SNOW, R. E. (1969) 'Individual differences in learning ability as a function of instructional variables', Final Report (contract OEC–4–6061269–1217) (Stanford University) *24, 25, 34*

DUNKIN, M. J. and BIDDLE, B. J. (1974) *The Study of Teaching* (Holt, Rinehart and Winston, New York) *11, 14–17, 31*

DUTHIE, J. H. (1970) *Primary School Survey* (H.M.S.O., Edinburgh) *44*

ENTWISTLE, N. J. (1972) 'Personality and academic attainment', *British Journal of Educational Psychology* 42, 137–51 *127, 128, 132*

FEATHERSTONE, J. (1967) 'Schools for children – what's happening in British classrooms', *New Republic*, 19 August 1967, 17–21 *8*

FISHER, E. J. (1972) *Learning how to Learn* (Harcourt, Brace, Jovanovich, New York) *8*

FLANDERS, N. A. (1965) 'Teacher influence, pupil attitudes and achievement', *Cooperative Research Monograph* 12 (Washington D.C. Office of Education) *29*

FLANDERS, N. A. (1970) *Analyzing Teacher Behaviour* (Addison-Wesley, Reading, Mass.) *14, 18, 19, 20, 30*

FLANDERS, N. A. and SIMON, A. (1969) 'Teacher effectiveness', in Ebel, R. L. (ed.), *Encyclopedia of Educational Research*, 1423–31 *17*

FROOME, S. (1974) 'Back on the right track', *Education* 3–13 2, 13–16 *93*

FROOME, S. (1975) 'Note of dissent', in Bullock Report (1975) *82, 162*

FURST, N. F. (1967) 'The multiple languages of the classroom: a further analysis and a synthesis of meanings communicated in high school teaching', unpublished doctoral dissertation (Temple University) *18*

GAGE, N. L. (1963) 'Paradigms for research on teaching', in Gage, N. L. (ed.), *Handbook of Research on Teaching* (Rand McNally, Chicago) *13*

GAGE, N. L. (1972) *Teacher Effectiveness and Teacher Education* (Pacific, Palo Alto) *12, 17*

GAGE, N. L. and UNRUH, W. R. (1967) 'Theoretical formulations for research on teaching', *Review of Educational Research* 37, 358–70 *11*

GARDNER, D. E. M. (1966) *Experiment and Tradition in Primary Schools* (Methuen, London) *26*

GETZELS, J. N. and THELEN, H. A. (1960) 'A conceptual framework for the study of the classroom group as a social system', in Morrison, A. and McIntyre, D. (1972) *Social Psychology of Teaching* (Penguin, Harmondsworth) *128*

GLASER, B. G. and STRAUSS, A. L. (1967) *The Discovery of Grounded Theory: Strategies for Qualitative Research* (Weidenfeld, New York) *31*

GOODLAD, J. I. (1969) Quoted in Silberman (1970) *3*

GRAHAM, P. A. (1967) *Progressive Education: From Arcady to Academe* (Teachers College Press, Columbia University) *2*

GRIMES, J. W. and ALLINSMITH, W. (1961) 'Compulsivity, anxiety and school achievement', *Merrill Palmer Quarterly* **7**, 247–71 *24–5*

GUGGENHEIM, F. (1961) 'Classroom climate and the learning of mathematics', *Arithmetic Teacher* **8**, 363–7 *23*

GUSTAFSSON, J. E. (1974) 'Verbal versus figural in aptitude-treatment interactions', Report No 36 (Institute of Education, University of Goteborg) *24*

HADOW REPORT (1931) *Report of the Consultative Committee on the Primary School* (H.M.S.O., London) *3–4, 37*

HADDON, F. A. and LYTTON, H. (1968) 'Teaching approach and the development of divergent thinking abilities in primary schools', *British Journal of Educational Psychology* **38**, 171–80 *26*

HARGREAVES, D. (1972) *Interpersonal Relations and Education* (Routledge and Kegan Paul, London) *53*

HARRIS, A. J., MORRISON, C., SERWER, B. L. and GOLD, L. (1968) 'A continuation of the CRAFT Project' (City University of New York, New York) *19*

HARRIS, A. J. and SERWER, B. L. (1966) 'Comparison of reading approaches in first grade teaching with disadvantaged children', Co-operative Research Project 2677, USOE (University of New York, New York) *19*

HAWKINS, D. (1966) 'Learning the unteachable', in Shulman and Keislar (1966) *10*

HERBERT, J. (1967) *A System of Analysing Lessons* (Teachers College Press, New York) *29*

HOLBROOK, D. (1961) *English in the Secondary School* (Cambridge University Press, Cambridge) *115*

HOURD, M. (1949) Quoted in Shayer (1972) *115*

HOWARTH, E. and BROWNE, J. A. (1971) 'An item factor analysis of the 16 P.F.', *Personality* **2**, 117–39 *128*

HOWARTH, E. and BROWNE, J. A. (1972) 'An item factor analysis of the Eysenck Personality Inventory', *British Journal of Social and Clinical Psychology* **11**, 162–74 *128*

HOWE, V. M. (1974) *Informal Teaching in the Open Classroom* (Macmillan, New York) *8*

JAYNE, C. D. (1945) 'A study of the relationship between teaching procedures and educational outcomes', *Journal of Experimental Education* **14**, 101–34 *14*

JOHNSON, B. and MCATHLONE, B. (1970) (eds) *Verdict on the Facts* (Advisory Centre for Education, Cambridge) *6–7*

JOHNSON, M. (1973) 'A skeptic's view', in Myers, D. A. and Myers, L. (eds) *Open Education Re-examined* (D. C. Heath, Lexington, Mass.) *7*

JORDAN, J. (in preparation) 'The structure and correlates of self concept in different types of primary classroom', unpublished Ph.D. thesis (University of Lancaster) *129, 131*

KENDLER, H. H. (1966) 'Reflections on the conference', in Shulman and Keislar (1966) *24*

KERLINGER, F. N. (1973) *Foundations of Behavioural Research* (Holt, Rinehart and Winston, New York) *53*

KIEREN, T. E. (1968) 'Activity learning', *Review of Educational Research* **39**, 509–22 *23*

KILPATRICK, W. H. (1918) 'The project method', *Teachers College Record* **19**, 319–35 *2*

LAHADERNE, H. M. (1968) 'Attitudinal and intellectual correlates of attention: a study of four sixth grade classrooms', *Journal of Educational Psychology* **59**, 320–4 *103, 159*

LANGDON, M. (1961) *Let the Children Write* (Longman, London) *116*

LA SHIER, W. S. and WESTMEYER, P. (1967) 'The use of interaction analysis in BSCS laboratory block classrooms', *Journal of Teacher Education* **18**, 435–45 *18*

LEESE, J. (1973) 'Origins and antecedents', in Myers, D. A. and Myers, L. *Open Education Re-examined* (D. C. Heath, Lexington, Mass.) *8*

LEITH, G. O. M. (1972) 'Personality, intellectual style and study background', *Mededeling* **14** (University of Utrecht) *25*

LEITH, G. O. M. and BOSSETT, R. (1967) 'Mode of learning and personality', Research Report No 14 (National Centre for Programmed Learning, University of Birmingham) *24*

LONG, G. (in preparation) 'Personality and classroom behaviour in the primary school', unpublished Ph.D. thesis (University of Lancaster) *129*

LOVELL, K. (1963) 'Informal versus formal education and reading attainments in the junior school', *Educational Research* **6**, 71–6 *26*

MARSH, J. E. and WILDER, E. W. (1954) 'Identifying the effective instructor: a review of the quantitative studies 1900–52', Research Bulletin No AFPTRC-TR-54-44, U.S.A.F. Personnel Training Research Center, San Antonio, Texas *13*

MARSHALL, S. (1966) *An Experiment in Education* (Cambridge University Press, Cambridge) *116*

McKINNEY, J. D., MASON, J., PERKERSON, K. and CLIFFORD, M. (1975) 'Relationship between behaviour and academic achievement', *Journal of Educational Psychology* **67**, 198–203 *103, 159*

McQUITTY, L. L. (1967) 'A mutual development of some typological theories and pattern analysis methods', *Educational and Psychological Measurements* **26**, 253–65 *45*

MAUDE, A. (1969) 'The egalitarian threat', in Cox and Dyson (1969a), 7–8 *6*

MEDLEY, D. M. (1972) 'Early history of research on teacher behaviour', *International Review of Education* **18**, 430–9 *11, 12, 13–14*

MEDLEY, D. M. and MITZEL, H. E. (1958) 'A technique for measuring classroom behaviour', *Journal of Educational Psychology* **49**, 86–92 *19*

MEDLEY, D. M. and MITZEL, H. E. (1959) 'Some behavioural correlates of teacher effectiveness', *Journal of Educational Psychology* **50**, 239–46 *19*

MEDLEY, D. M. and MITZEL, H. E. (1963) 'Measuring classroom behaviour by systematic observation', in Gage, N. L. (ed.), *Handbook of Research on Teaching* (Rand McNally, Chicago) *13*

MINUCHIN, P., BIBER, B., SHAPIRO, E. and ZIMILES, H. (1969) *The Psychological Impact of School Experience* (Basic Books, New York) *25–6, 28, 131*

MISCHEL, W. (1968) *Personality and Assessment* (Wiley, New York) *127*

MITZEL, H. E. (1957) 'A behavioural approach to the assessment of teacher effectiveness', unpublished report, City of New York College, New York *14–17*

MORRISON, A. and McINTYRE, D. (1967) 'Changes in opinion about education during the first year of teaching', *British Journal of Social and Clinical Psychology* **6**, 161–3 *55*

MORRISON, A. and McINTYRE, D. (1969) *Teachers and Teaching* (Penguin, Harmondsworth) *127*

NUTHALL, G. (1968) 'Studies of teaching: types of research on teaching', *New Zealand Journal of Educational Studies* **3**, 125–47 *31*

NUTHALL, G. and SNOOK, I. (1973) 'Contemporary models of teaching', in Travers, R. M. W. (ed.) *Second Handbook of Research on Teaching* (Rand McNally, New York) *31*

OLANDER, H. T. and ROBERTSON, H. C. (1973) 'The effectiveness of discovery and expository methods in the teaching of fourth grade mathematics', *Journal for Research in Mathematics Education* **4**, 33–44 *23–4, 27–8*

PETERS, R. S. (1969) (ed.) *Perspectives on Plowden* (Routledge and Kegan Paul, London) *5, 10*

PETERSON, D. R. (1965) 'Scope and generality of verbally defined personality factors', *Psychological Review* **72**, 48–59 *128*

PETERSON, W. A. (1964) 'Age, teacher's role and the institutional setting', in Biddle, B. J. and Ellena, W. J. (eds), *Contemporary Research on Teacher Effectiveness* (Holt, Rinehart and Winston, New York) *55*

PLOWDEN REPORT (1967) *Children and their Primary Schools*, report of the Central Advisory Council for Education (England) (H.M.S.O., London) *viii, xi, 4, 5, 9, 37, 39, 54, 67, 88, 93, 115, 149, 150, 153*

PLOWDEN, LADY (1973) 'Aims in primary education', *Education* 3–13 **1**, 89–90 *163*

POWELL, E. (1968) 'Teacher behaviour and pupil achievement', *Classroom Interaction Newsletter* **3**, 3–5 *18–19*

PLUCKROSE, H. (1975) 'Openness is all', *Times Educational Supplement* (10 October 1975), 21 *160*

RATHBONE, C. H. (1971) *Open Education – The Informal Classroom* (Citation Press, New York) *8, 40*

RICHARDS, C. (1974) 'Curriculum development in the English primary school – reality and possibility', *Elementary School Journal* **74**, 211–19 *7*

RICHARDS, P. N. and BOLTON, N. (1971) 'Divergent thinking, mathematical ability and type of mathematics teaching in junior school children', *British Journal of Educational Psychology* **41**, 32–7 *26, 28, 152*

ROGERS, V. R. (1970) *Teaching in the British Primary Schools* (Macmillan, New York) *8, 54*

ROSENSHINE, B. (1970) 'Evaluation of classroom instruction', *Review of Educational Research* **40**, 279–300 *17*

ROSENSHINE, B. (1971) *Teaching Behaviours and Student Achievement* (N.F.E.R., Slough) *17, 18*

ROSENSHINE, B. and FURST, N. F. (1973) 'The use of direct observation to study teaching', in Travers, R. M. W. (ed.), *Second Handbook of Research on Teaching* (Rand McNally, Chicago) *17, 31, 33*

ROTHKOPF, E. Z. (1970) 'The concept of mathmagenic activities', *Review of Educational Research* 40, 325–36 *158*

ROWE, A. (1967) *English through Experience* (Oxford University Press, London) *116*

RUBINSTEIN, D. and STONEMAN, C. (1970) (eds) *Education for Democracy* (Penguin Education Special, London) *6–7*

RYANS, D. G. (1960) *Characteristics of Teachers* (American Council on Education, Washington, D.C.) *55*

SAMUELS, S. J. and TURNURE, J. E. (1974) 'Attention and reading achievement in first grade boys and girls', *Journal of Educational Psychology* 66, 29–32 *103, 159*

SAX, O. and OTTINA, J. R. (1958) 'The arithmetic achievement of pupils differing in school experience', *California Journal of Educational Research* 9, 15–19 *23, 28*

SCHANTZ, B. B. (1963) 'An experimental study comparing the effects of verbal recall with children in a direct and indirect teaching method using the Flanders categories of interaction analysis as a tool of measurement', unpublished thesis (University of Pennsylvania) *19*

SELLS, S. B. (1963) 'Approaches to the taxonomy of social situations', Technical Report No 4 (O.N.R.) *33, 128*

SELLS, S. B. (1973) 'Prescriptions for a multivariate model in personality and psychological theory', in Royce, J. R. (ed.), *Multivariate Analysis and Psychological Theory* (Academic Press, New York) *128, 157*

SHERMAN, V. S. (1970) *Two contrasting educational models: applications and policy implications* (Stanford Research Institute, Menlo Park, California) *37*

SHAYER, D. (1972) *The Teaching of English in Schools, 1900–1970* (Routledge and Kegan Paul, London) *115*

SHULMAN, L. S. and KEISLAR, E. R. (1966) (eds) *Learning by Discovery: A Critical Appraisal* (Rand McNally, Chicago)

SIEGEL, L. and SIEGEL, L. C. (1967) 'The instructional gestalt', in Siegel, L. (ed.), *Instruction: Some Contemporary Viewpoints* (Chandler, San Francisco) *30*

SILBERMAN, C. E. (1970) *Crisis in the Classroom* (Random House, New York) *8–9, 54, 150*

SIMON, B. (1972) 'The nature of classroom learning in primary schools', S.S.R.C. Report HR 291 *39, 54*

SNOW, R. E. (1973) 'Theory construction for research on teaching', in Travers, R. M. W. (ed.), *Second Handbook For Research on Teaching* (Rand McNally, Chicago) *32*

SOAR, R. S. (1966) 'An integrative approach to classroom learning', ERIC document ED 033 749 *20*

SOAR, R. S. (1967) 'Whither research on teacher behaviour?', *Classroom Interaction Newsletter* 3, 9–11 *29–30, 32, 33*

SOAR, R. S. (1972) 'Teacher behaviour related to pupil growth', *International Review of Education* 18, 508–25 *20–2, 33, 81*

SOLOMON, D. and KENDALL, A. J. (1975) 'Individual characteristics and children's performance in open and traditional classes', paper read at A.E.R.A. annual conference, Washington *153*

SOUTHGATE, V. (1973) 'Reading: three to thirteen', *Education 3–13*, 1, 47–52
162

STAKE, R. E. (1970) 'The decision: does classroom observation belong in an
evaluative plan?', in Gallagher, J. J., Nuthall, G. A. and Rosenshine, B.
(eds) *Classroom Observation* (Rand McNally, Chicago)   *33*

STATHAM, M. (1976) 'The development of the mechanical accuracy measure',
mimeograph (Department of Educational Research, University of Lancaster)   *121*

STEPHENS, J. M. (1967) *The Process of Schooling: A Psychological Examination*
(Holt, Rinehart and Winston, New York)   *13*

STEPHENS, L. S. (1974) *The Teacher's Guide to Open Education* (Holt, Rinehart
and Winston, New York)   *8, 9*

STONES, E. (1973) 'Voyage of discovery', *Education 3–13*, 1, 18–22   *29*

TAYLOR, J. (1971) *Organising and Integrating the Infant Day* (George Allen and
Unwin, London)   *161–2*

TAYLOR, P. H. and HOLLEY, B. J. (1975) 'A study of the emphasis given by
teachers of different age groups to aims in primary education', in Taylor,
P. H. (ed.) *Aims Influence and Change in the Primary School Curriculum*
(N.F.E.R., Slough)   *56–8*

THOMPSON, G. R. and BOWERS, N. G. (1968) 'Fourth grade achievement as
related to creativity, intelligence and teaching style', paper presented to
A.E.R.A. conference, Chicago   *19*

TRAVERS, R. M. W. (1971) 'Some further reflections on the nature of a theory
of instruction', in Westbury, I. and Bellack, A. A. (eds), *Research into Classroom Processes* (Teachers College Press, New York)   *29*

TREW, K. (1974) 'Classroom practices in the upper primary school', internal
report (Northern Ireland Council for Educational Research, Belfast)
150

TROWN, E. A. (1973) 'An investigation of structural approaches to the teaching of mathematics in relation to dimensions of pupil personality', unpublished D.Phil. thesis (University of Sussex)   *24, 25*

TUPPEN, C. J. S. (1965) 'The measurement of teachers' attitudes', *Educational
Research* 8, 142–5   *55*

TURNER, R. L. and DENNY, D. A. (1969) 'Teacher characteristics, teacher
behaviour, and changes in pupil creativity', *Elementary School Journal* 69,
265–70   *20*

WADE, B. (in preparation) 'Anxiety and motivation in relation to pupil
behaviour in formal and informal classrooms', unpublished Ph.D. thesis
(University of Lancaster)   *103–5, 129*

WALBERG, H. J. and THOMAS, S. C. (1971) 'Characteristics of open education:
towards an operational definition', Report to U.S. Office of Education No
OEC-1-7-062805-3936   *39, 40–1*

WALLEN, N. E. (1966) 'Relations between teacher characteristics and student
behaviour: Part III', Co-op Research Project 2628 (USOE, Salt Lake City,
University of Utah)   *19*

WALLEN, N. E. and TRAVERS, N. W. (1963) 'Analysis and investigation of
teaching methods', in Gage, N. L. (ed.) *Handbook of Research on Teaching*
(Rand McNally, Chicago)   *13–14, 22–3, 28*

WALSH, J. H. (1965) *Teaching English* (University of London Press, London) *116*

WARD, W. D. and BARCHER, P. R. (1975) 'Reading achievement and creativity as related to open classroom experience', *Journal of Educational Psychology* **67**, 683–91 *153*

WEBER, L. (1971) *The English Infant School and Informal Education* (Prentice Hall, Englewood Cliffs, New Jersey) *8*

WEBER, W. A. (1968) 'Relationship between teacher behaviour and pupil creativity in the elementary school', paper presented at A.E.R.A. meeting, Chicago *18–19*

WHITEHEAD, F. (1966) *The Disappearing Dais* (Chatto and Windus, London) *115*

WILEY, D. E. and HARNISHFEGER, A. (1975) 'Distinct pupils, distinctive schooling: individual differences in exposure to instructional activities', paper read at A.E.R.A. annual conference, Washington *159*

WITTROCK, M. C. (1966) 'The learning by discovery hypothesis', in Shulman and Keislar (1966) *10*

WODTKE, K. H. and WALLEN, N. E. (1965) 'The effects of teacher control in the classroom on pupils' creativity test gains', *American Educational Research Journal* **2**, 75–82 *19–20*

YOUNG, M. (1965) *Innovation and Research in Education* (Routledge and Kegan Paul, London) *1*

Subject index